GAIA VILLAGE

Creating a community by embodying true self

BOOK 1

Dismantle Your Illusions

Saeko Angwin

First published by Busybird Publishing 2025

Copyright © 2025 Saeko Angwin

ISBN:
Paperback: 978-1-923216-98-3
Ebook: 978-1-923216-99-0

This work is copyright. Apart from any use permitted under the *Copyright Act 1968*, no part of this publication may be reproduced, stored in a retrieval system or transmitted in any form or by any means, electronic, mechanical, photocopying, recording or otherwise, without the prior written permission of Saeko Angwin.

The information in this book is based on the author's experiences and opinions. The author and publisher disclaim responsibility for any adverse consequences, which may result from use of the information contained herein. Permission to use any external content has been sought by the author. Any breaches will be rectified in further editions of the book.

Cover Image: 'Be Your True Colours' painting by Saeko Angwin

Cover design: Busybird Publishing

Layout and typesetting: Busybird Publishing

Busybird Publishing
2/118 Para Road
Montmorency, Victoria
Australia 3094
www.busybird.com.au

Short Description of Gaia Village

Saeko has an unwavering spirit and has been determined to discover her true self. She has transformed relationship experiences with her family, friends, spiritualists and communities into wisdom. Her relentless inquiry and curiosity about life's mysteries, even in the most trying situations, have opened the door to receive messages from herself, the creator of HER universe. Despite her challenges, she continued to seek convincing information that could apply to everyone. As a result, she has gained insight into the creator's intentions behind all the events. *Gaia Village* represents the culmination of her inquiries, with all the messages addressing why we struggle to perceive the truth.

This book seeks to understand the old illusory world by exploring the illusory self that was shaped by our traumas. Therefore, it does not pursue 'justice', which serves only our illusions and does not grant us freedom. Self-exploration, introspection and self-expansion with the eyes of innocence and curiosity allow us to uncover who we truly are. Embodying one's true self by self-healing creates your new world: this is a pathway to *Gaia Village*, a new community.

Contents

Acknowledgement	1
The Purpose	3
Defining Invaders	5
Chapter 1 - Loss of Self-Trust	**7**
Introduction	9
Once Upon a Time… the Memory of Who We Truly Are	12
Our Trauma	13
Ego and Its Needs	14
Male and Female Energies and Inner Child	16
Our Natural Self	18
Fear of Ourselves and Loss of Self-Trust	20
Chapter 2 - The Effect of Our Traumas	**21**
Warrior Energy	23
Grief Is Relief: Returned Soldiers	25
Our Long Healing Journey	27
Problem, Reaction and Solution Program	29
Projection of Abuser, Victim and Saviour Program	31
Why History Repeats Itself	34
No One Can Stop the Life Force	36
Chapter 3 - What We Believed To Be True	**37**
Illusion of Ownership	39
Money	41
Hierarchy of Power to Communities Without Hierarchy	44
The Limitation of Knowledge and Teaching	48
No Middle Man	52
Our Inner Intelligence vs Legal System in the Old World	54
Chapter 4 - Beyond Illusional Collective Consciousness	**57**
Fear Attracts the Fearful: How to Deal With Your 'Enemy'	59
Beyond Illusional Collective Consciousness	63

Shame and Guilt to the Illusional Collective Consciousness	65
Loyalty to the Illusional Collective Consciousness as Survival	67
Seeking the Truth/Justice to Compensate Injustice	68
'I Deserve Success!': Success Becomes Justice as Revenge	70

Chapter 5 - Blindspot of Spiritualists – The Wounded: Healers, Psychics, Shamans and Spiritual 'Leaders' — 73

Bringing Your Power Back	75
Trauma of Spiritualists – Healers, Shamans and Spiritual Leaders	76
Self-Abandonment	77
Extreme Loyalty to the Illusional Collective Consciousness	79
Self-Belief: 'I am the Darkness'	81
'Healing' Others by Shame and Guilt of Healers and Shamans	84
Wounded Inner Child of Spiritualists	88
'Hope' and 'Faith' as Justification for Constant Sufferings	90
'Shaman': Elite Official Slaves Who Serve 'God'	92
Fear of Innocence; Fear of Freedom; Fear of Ourselves	94
The One Who Embodies the Truth	96

Chapter 6 - What Can We Do? — 101

Self-Value and Self-Appreciation	103
Peace and Balance	105
Abundance At All Times: Infinite Possibility	107
Creating Your World, Not Changing the World	109
Manifesting Yourself	111
Everything and Everybody Are You in Your World	112
Heaven is Here	114

In Summary	116
Bio - Saeko Angwin	119

Acknowledgement

I want to express my deep gratitude to my family – Paul, Mateo and Isa – and my friends. You have been committed to uncovering the voices of your true selves. In my soul, I heard your strong desire to listen to your own voice, and I genuinely wished to do the same. In the face of the unknown, our perseverance and self-trust shone like a light in the darkness for each other.

Mum and Dad, your unwavering presence revealed my blind spots and mirrored the dynamics of my unconscious behaviours, helping me to understand and heal myself.

Ancestors, I have felt everything you experienced, even though you have all passed on and are no longer here physically. I felt your pain and hope as my own. We are ending all the pain and struggles of the family line, bringing us peace.

I will not name the spiritualists I encountered – healers, shamans, psychics and spiritual leaders. I was initially drawn to and admired your magician-like abilities, spiritual teachings and courage because I didn't trust myself. I did not believe I could heal myself, and you may have also thought everyone needed you for healing.

Due to the shared resonance of trauma and the lack of self-trust in self-healing, we have come together again in this lifetime to recognise our pain. As a result, it is your trauma, rather than your teaching, healing or psychic abilities, that has revealed my unconscious trauma through our relationships.

Because of this realisation, I stopped relying on you for my healing. I began to trust myself, discovered my gifts and was able to reconnect with myself as the creator and write this book. I admit that I sometimes put you on a pedestal, and I owe you an apology for that. At the same time, I am grateful that we found each other again and that I freed myself from this co-dependency. We are here to liberate ourselves from the co-dependency between healers and those who want to be healed. We are here to dismantle this paradigm and give birth to something new.

Finally, I am truly grateful to my husband, Paul, who has held my hand throughout our healing journey. Our incredible perseverance and curiosity have brought us to a new world.

Without your love and dedicated support, I would not have been able to give a birth to *Gaia Village*.

The Purpose

We are returning to a new world where we express our true selves. Our inner child, the core energy that initially created Gaia, revives and leads in creating it this time again.

For that, we will first destroy the illusions that kept us in the old world, where we consider ourselves incomplete and inadequate, co-created by our traumatised selves and the invaders.

The world where we are going is unknown, and no books or texts have been written on creating a new world. It is a blank paper; you write it down as you go. We are here to experience ourselves. The experience of your world is the experience of YOU. No one else creates your world but you. This time, the difference is, unlike the old illusional world of survival, ownership, hierarchy and co-dependency, we are free to create as we wish with our authenticity of abundance, bliss and innocence.

This book describes the illusional collective consciousness created by our trauma in great detail. It is more like the history of humanity, and we are the living history itself. And all the information about our history is in us.

Dismantling self-deceptions by finding and understanding the trauma hidden behind them is a necessary process for creating a new world of your natural self. This requires unrelenting observation, especially SELF-observation.

Even though the ego – the illusional self – was created due to our trauma, we often criticise our ego instead of paying attention to what it is trying to say. Self-criticism is self-torture. By doing so, we hurt ourselves even more, and the traumatised self is left alone, ignored, and not understood and empathised. Instead, we all project our self-judgment onto others, so living in this world is challenging.

Understanding the illusion of ourselves will help us find and eventually heal our trauma. By doing so, we can also disconnect from the illusional collective consciousness created by our egos. As a by-product, we learn the illusion of the invaders' power and how they used their projection to influence us.

In other words, the information provided here is for you to get to know your ego, which has been speaking on behalf of your trauma and asking for your attention to understand its story. Eventually, we allow them to heal by listening and empathising with our own wounds.

In each section, you can discover self-illusions and understand how they currently play out in any area of your life: relationships with your family members, friends, school, work, business, community and all other domains.

Please focus on your feelings triggered by the content or words in this book – journey with them to wherever they take you. They will help you discover the root of your trauma. Follow your heart and allow it to speak up to discover the time and event you began to perceive yourself as incomplete and inadequate. Do not dismiss even subtle emotions during the journey. This is the journey to embody your true self hidden behind your trauma.

Continuous self-healing opens the door to our natural self, the new world, and we do it individually. After all, we are all on the same journey of self-manifestation, but we live in individual worlds. Therefore, we are experiencing the unique you.

The descriptions of the illusions in this book come from my personal experiences throughout my lifetimes and what I shared with my ancestors. Through healing, I opened the doors to that wisdom. If I had not experienced them in any lifetimes, I would not have been

The Purpose

able to gain the information. In other words, if I had not been healed, I would not have been able to receive them. Therefore, it differs from accessing only knowledge through channelling without my actual experience. This is not just knowledge without an information receiver's experience. It is wisdom that is backed up by experience.

The information in *Gaia Village* will ensure that you are creating something new from your natural state, not repeatedly from the same old illusions. This book will allow you to recognise the old pattern of yourself and birth your new world.

The creator of your world is, has been, and will always be you, even though we co-created the old world with the invaders in the past. Creation was always on our side. That is the power that you are! We are going back home, *Gaia Village!*

Defining Invaders

As you read Gaia Village, you might wonder, 'Who are the invaders?'

They are non-physical beings. I do not know their name. They influence people's minds by projecting who they are onto us. Their existence in us is evident since many of us struggle to be who we truly are due to their synthetic nature. What hinders our authenticity is the mind program. It is the illusions co-created with the invaders by self-perception as incomplete and inadequate.

They invaded Gaia and began controlling our minds so we would stop listening to our hearts and inner child. They are the masters of illusions, latching onto our creation and co-creating with our ego illusions of survival, ownership, hierarchy and co-dependency. They are very good at keeping our minds occupied with illusions so that we do not remember we are the power, the creator of our worlds. They have divided our way of life into business, politics, communication, academics, education, entertainment, medicine and other sectors. They have created a system and structure to operate their agenda by giving a sense of superiority and privileges to people at the top of the hierarchy in each industry.

This book does not detail them because it only focuses on what illusions we have about ourselves and encourages you to discover and understand your trauma. The more we pay attention to invaders and what they do to us, the more we are drawn into their energy and seek 'justice' or blame them for our misery. This leads us further away from self-healing and creating our lives, resulting instead in another form of suffering through relentless self-attack. We can never embody the truth by blaming 'the enemy' and seeking justice.

The essence of this book lies in our self-understanding and encourages self-healing, which is even more challenging and rewarding. The focus is on us. As a by-product of understanding the illusions and trauma, you will learn the invaders' projections and how they operate.

By dismantling our illusional selves, we will know, feel, and be the truth – the creator who created everything in your world.

Chapter 1

Loss of Self-Trust

Introduction

We know the world of abundance, bliss and innocence because it is our natural state, as we experienced it as children, and it exists deep in our souls. Our blueprint of the new world lies in the home within ourselves, where our inner child comes out and plays.

We may not clearly remember the inner home and how to get back there, but we know we can bring it into existence as long as we exist here because it is in us, not outside us. We are the blueprint self.

We can access all the information and wisdom to create it because we innately have them all. Its vision of our inner child is the one we are creating physically on this earth – Gaia: we embody it.

How do I know that we embody it? Because we innately know all that beauty of our home. We created it a very, very long time ago, and we have memories of it. Even our minds forgot it, but our inner child remembers it all, what it was like. If we did not have a reference to it, then we would not have struggled and suffered in the old world of survival that much. In other words, we had been deeply hurt because of the memories.

'I know the earth and humanity are abundant and full of possibilities, and I feel so safe there, but the world I am physically experiencing is the opposite of it; rather, challenge after challenge. Why?'

While I experienced the old survival world, I looked for the beautiful world I saw in my vision, thinking it was outside myself and already existed somewhere in Gaia. However, I could not find it in my home and Japan, so I left my country to find it somewhere. I could not find it anywhere. So, I believed someone else who was charismatic and gifted would come out and create it for me. Even though I waited for them to appear, they never came... Then I realised it does not exist anywhere in the world. I need to manifest my home, my world where my inner child can play if I want to live. I need to bring it into existence. No one else can do it for me. It is truly individual work.

I was determined to dismantle all the elements that prevented me from creating a new world that is the manifestation of my authentic self, without knowing how reckless I was. For that, I needed to dive into my hidden traumas and illusions. Behind all this, there was a powerful force to push forward. It was my inner child. I had no choice but to listen to my inner child's desire. What can I do? It is so powerful! It is far more potent than my trauma and illusions.

I tell you, it was a bloody rocky journey! I could not blame anyone for my inability to self-heal because not being able to heal is a choice, and the truth is everyone can heal! Although I did, at times, blame people around me when it was unbearable.

I know, and you know, our journey has been highly challenging. Especially we who listen to our inner child that has been disappointed, hurt, saddened and in pain because we believe in illusions and deception. Despite this, if we live on the earth, every one of us voluntarily maintains and recreates the mind program – that is, the illusions – that does not allow us to see the truth about us as the creators due to our trauma.

The moment has arrived for us to come out and express who we truly are by letting our wild inner child be released from their limitations. Eventually, there will be no more survival or hiding if you choose to.

Each of us is on a unique path and is in different stages of the same journey – a journey back to our natural state. Hence, individual healing will continue, and everyone will begin to manifest the abundance, bliss and innocence that we are.

Gaia Village describes all the illusions we have believed in that undermine our creative force. So ask yourself,

'Do I believe in this illusion? Then what happened for me to believe so?'

Releasing our inner child liberates the energy that created Gaia before the invasion. That is where we restart our evolution after long, repetitive stagnation. We are reconnecting the energetic force. We are going home and restarting to continue to evolve.

Gaia Village is about what to let go of to bring back your most potent inner child's energy to create your new world on Gaia.

Once Upon a Time… the Memory of Who We Truly Are

Once upon a time, we knew we were connected to nature: plants, trees, insects, animals, microorganisms and everything. We treated them with respect because they were us, and we were aware and conscious of them as us. We did not force anything or anybody to do something because there was no hierarchy in the importance of all existence. I use 'we' because our trauma and illusions apply to our ancestors, us in past and present lives, and the collective consciousness.

Due to the connection with all that is, we did not know we were lacking. We knew we were 'enough'. We did not have to worry about the future because we knew we embodied our abundance and bliss. We effortlessly manifested everything we wanted to experience. We did not have the concept of ownership because we could create everything from ourselves infinitely.

The creation was for the experience, not to own what we created because owning would have stopped creation. We knew we had the power to create anything. 'So why do we need to own when we can create any time we want?'

We knew we had created this world, so we trusted ourselves. Because of our self-trust, we trusted others, everything around us, and life itself. How could you not trust them? After all, they were all manifestations of ourselves.

Our Trauma

We have the eternal questions of 'who are we?' and 'why are we here?'

'How did we become enslaved from birth to death?' and 'what the hell happened?' These questions remain in us for our whole life. Some people even lost the ability to ask questions. We just accepted being a slave for survival, knowingly and unknowingly.

We want to remember where the feeling of loss comes from to know who we truly are. We have searched for answers to where this sense of loss comes from – 'What did we lose?' – not only in this lifetime but throughout many lifetimes.

We feel whole when our male, female and inner child energies communicate well. However, foreign substances have invaded our consciousness and influenced our mind, male energy, to believe in illusions and disconnect him from the heart, which is female energy, and inner child energy. We have started to perceive ourselves as incomplete and inadequate and have lost self-trust. Because of this disconnection, we have always felt we need something or someone else to feel whole; co-dependency was introduced. They influence people's minds by projecting what they are as parasites that require a host onto us. Their existence in our minds has made us struggle to be who we truly are as the creators of our lives.

We were called to self-healing to embody our authenticity. Each one of us embarks on waking ourselves up individually.

For healing, we are required to trace back to the incident to understand our trauma. When you get triggered, follow whatever feelings and emotions arise, because they hold all the clues to comprehend it. Following what our hearts express would help us return to the root of our wounds. It is crucial to sit with these emotions. For myself, I imagine sitting on them as if they were a magic carpet and letting them take me on a journey through whole emotional ups and downs, from the trigger point of the trauma. Hold on tight, as you will relive the traumatic experience, which can be very unpleasant. However, this process will allow healing to occur.

Some say we planned traumas to learn from suffering. However, we did not create the pain and hurt because we wanted to experience the suffering. We did not come here to experience that as an objective. Instead, for self-discovery, we chose to understand the root of our trauma and dismantle the illusions that we have created based on the wounds. This is all to recall and embody your true self hidden behind the trauma. This is healing. It is as if you are digging out the gold that is YOU buried in trauma, so if you want to bring it back to you, then facing your trauma is inevitable.

Ego and Its Needs

Our natural state is abundant, blissful and innocent. However, due to our trauma, we created an ego, which is an illusional self, to cope in the old system of survival, hierarchy and co-dependency. Ego, the identity that our mind created, was made based on the self-belief as one who is incomplete and inadequate. Our existence needs protection, and for that, we must rely on something and someone else who is more 'capable' than us. It wants to have 'safety', but it keeps choosing fake 'safety' by someone, system and structure that appears to provide that. However, this fake protection and safety fit into where we feel vulnerable, coming from the lack and incompleteness, because those feelings are also perceptions and are simply not true.

Even though our sole purpose of ego was made to protect ourselves from outside attacks, in reality, ego was not quite able to execute its purpose because it also suppressed and attacked the vulnerabilities of our hearts and the innocence of our inner child.

However, without ego, we felt danger in the old world. Ego did the same as the invaders.

We are taught to disguise our egos as something defiled. For the entirety of our lives, we learn to criticise ego as if we are torturing ourselves. The attack we thought came from outside that we needed to protect ourselves from was mostly self-attack. This is exactly what I mean by we keep living in the 'effect' of trauma. We are frozen in the time when we had been traumatised, and we continue to live with the thought of being attacked. Thus, we live in fear 24/7. At the same time, the vibration of the ego, which is incomplete and inadequate, was a signal lamp that attracted invaders' continuous vibrational attacks to keep us in the vibrational field of fear.

The ego's needs and wants stem from trauma, from feelings of lack and imperfection. We always try to own or bring something outside ourselves to fill in what we think is missing.

The more we seek to 'own' things outside ourselves – driven by our needs and wants – the more we reinforce the illusion of ownership. No matter what we get, we never feel whole. Only the emptiness of ownership remains.

We can never feel complete by seeking fulfilment outside ourselves, because what we genuinely want is the wholeness that comes from reconnecting with our natural state. What we lack is not possessions, but the truth that we are already abundant, blissful and whole. Judging or ignoring our ego does not allow us to heal our trauma – the belief that we are not enough and incomplete due to the pain and hurt. Instead, understanding it will help us let the thought go and allow our natural state to emerge. Remember, our ego stems from trauma, and it tries to protect our vulnerability and innocence. Therefore, if we judge our ego, we are attacking and bullying our traumatised selves again and again: it is a self-torture program. We are letting go of the program by understanding our trauma and its mechanism.

Male and Female Energies and Inner Child

We are nothingness, and simultaneously, we are everything! Not just everything – infinite possibilities.

The belly button, where our inner child resides, is the energy of abundance, bliss and innocence.

The inner child is curious and wants to experience beyond right and wrong or good and bad. There is no 'mistake' for it because all it is after is experience. That is why we can keep walking even if we 'fall' because whatever it experiences is just an experience. It is the source of intuition and the driving force behind our creations and evolution, diving into the unknown. It contributes new experiences to the mind, the body and the heart.

It is abundant because it is the driving force for unlimited experiences.

It is blissful because it is the life force and joy of aliveness.

It is innocence because it is our essence, the most precious thing we want to protect fiercely. Only innocence can tell what is an illusion and what is true. Innocence was considered sacred in the primordial before the invaders introduced various beliefs because it is the state of no self-doubt.

It is the most 'indomitable spirit' without knowing it is. It is just diving into another 'experience'. You can identify this energy in yourself. You never lose it.

The heart represents female energy and is an emotional navigator that decodes what the inner child wants, as a mother does to her child by feeling into her child's needs and wants. She helps her child's desires materialise by letting the male energy know through her feelings and emotions, representing the inner child.

The mind and the body, which are male energy, decode what the heart wants to say and, with the heart's assistance, help physically manifest what the inner child wants. The inner child communicates what it wants to experience with the mind through the heart. Those three parties express themselves through what they are good at.

Your inner child expresses a desire for experience, and your heart speaks vulnerabilities to ensure that the inner child's wishes are communicated to the mind and the body to bring into physical existence. This way of three-party communication for the co-creative process is living.

However, the inner child lost the connection with the female and male energies due to trauma. Our male energy operated everything dominantly by suppressing female energy and the inner child by believing that he was protecting them. Because our mind listened to the illusions for their survival instead of the heart and inner child, our heart could not express itself due to the fear of control by the mind, and the heart was not present with the inner child without feeling safe with the mind and the body. Without the connection with the male and female energies, the inner child was left alone without the help of the two because it had no support to manifest what it wanted or dreamed of. The inner child forgot who it was. It simply became a copy of the dynamics between male and female energies. This means that when it loses support, it loses vitality and aliveness as a child. It lost its sense of self and shut down, and it could no longer tell or know what it wanted, which is the driving force for infinite experience. What is more, it forgot its power of innocence. Eventually, it sometimes went wild out of despair without any support and even self-blame of the disharmony of the mind and heart to the point of polarising itself to the extreme opposites of the two and trying to fix it for them.

Our Natural Self

In the nothingness, we got bored, and curiosity about what we were and what we could do was born. We wanted to experience ourselves, so we created various experiences to know who we were. We were honest about and responded to our curiosity without any doubt or hesitation, with no time delay. The curiosity and innocence of self-trust could manifest everything instantly. Everything is a manifestation of ourselves. There is no ownership in our relationships with anything.

Our natural selves do not care about ownership because we know we create everything in our world, and we are abundant, blissful and innocent.

Because we are innately abundant, we suffer from or do not quite fit into the world of survival, hierarchy, co-dependency and ownership.

Because we are blissful, we get bored, and some of us cannot stand stagnation and repetition without creating new experiences.

Because we are innocent, we suffer self-doubt from not listening to and responding to our curiosity to create new experiences.

What hinders us from manifesting freedom of expression in creating experiences leads to our strong desire for freedom. This desire represents our memories of our true selves and shows how much we want to return to our original selves. It has nothing to do with the idea that owning more will free you. We cannot own experience because experiences are eternally born.

Realising our desire for freedom involves acknowledging our fear of releasing our egos' needs. Overcoming this fear can be challenging because expressing our free will appears to attack our and others' egos.

We allow our true selves to emerge by understanding and letting go of the trauma that created the old world. This is the road to knowing you can manifest your abundant, blissful and innocent world. Being the true self means trusting ourselves. Trusting ourselves means having no belief. We are free. You can create a world from your true essence, not the trauma.

Fear of Ourselves and Loss of Self-Trust

Throughout human history, we have continuously fought. Without violence and war, we can no longer even talk about our past. Even if the war starts with self-protection, harming the enemy, who also has loved ones, is not a good enough reason to justify what we have committed against them. What we have done to protect our loved ones costs too much already. Our minds try to make sense of what we do for survival. However, with our hearts and essence, we cannot comprehend what we do at all: we feel harming and killing people is just wrong, even for self-defence. It means that the conqueror and the loser both lose in the battle. Nobody wins a war.

We become fearful of ourselves and others because we all have done anything to win for our survival. This results in self-despair and a loss of self-trust. The most significant loss of humanity is that we cannot trust ourselves as innocent, abundant, blissful and, after all, sacred beings.

We cannot bear the pain again. When we connect with and love people, we believe we might hurt them or get hurt by them. This is because we think we all have the potential to harm others due to our self-belief as 'impure' beings. We tell ourselves and others, 'Don't trust ourselves and others because we have evil within.' The ones who trust themselves and others are considered naive. We all consume our time and energy to protect ourselves from possible hurt.

Hence, we choose not to communicate or interact authentically. We only share superficially or interact to the extent that we do not hurt ourselves and others, even with our loved ones. The lack of self-trust leads to disconnection with others and the collectives, and we all become lonely and isolated: we choose to become hermits, collectively.

Chapter 2

The Effect of Our Traumas

Warrior Energy

Warrior energy can be described as determination, discipline and a strong focus on protecting loved ones – the characteristics that are mainly used for battles.

'Why do we feel we have to fight for our lives?'

'Why do we always feel we must defend and protect ourselves and our loved ones by fighting?'

After all, 'What exactly are we protecting and from whom?'

If we did not experience defeat, we would not know what it is like to be defeated. It meant slavery for our whole lives and losing our human dignity and the sense of aliveness, lushness and, after all, freedom to live as we choose. Humanity has kept fighting because we do not want to feel the same pain, even though we have already experienced the trauma.

Throughout history, fighting has been our way of life. We physically fought in the war and later financially fought for survival. We fought for our family, children and ourselves for survival.

We thought the world was dangerous and our family was in danger. Men needed to be strong to protect women's vulnerability and our children's innocence. The exact same thing was happening inside us: we were trying to protect the innocence of our inner child and the vulnerability of our hearts. We all were warriors with and without choice.

We were alert 24/7. Sometimes, we attacked our enemy before we got attacked out of fear that we might experience the pain again. Even only by the thought of possibly being attacked, we were already in a combat state. We lived to prepare to avoid the tragedy of a possible attack. We were in a state of paranoia, almost, but that's what trauma does.

We lost trust in ourselves and life. For survival, we thought we needed to sacrifice everything we had. We ran the warrior program self-sufficiently and were busy participating in it. We were a slave to the program. All the invaders did was keep giving the masses fear to the extent that the self-sufficient warrior program kept running. We continuously ran the program because we believed it to be true.

We did not even know what we were fighting for anymore. The ones who lost their purpose of fighting became a danger to everybody. We fought for the sake of battle – the fight without a purpose turned into just violence. The victim by the perpetrator became the perpetrator, and this became a chain of violence.

Our warrior energy was used to maintain the invaders' power and control. They wanted us to consume our energy to fight for our survival. In fact, we kept this warrior program running because we could not let go of our fear. Therefore, we live in a world that we created based on fear.

I often felt attacked from outside: the invaders, people's criticism or judgment, and constant unexpected incidents. I needed to protect myself and my family from possible financial, relational and societal dangers. I was alert, even though people were living in their own self-torturing/judgmental world and projected it onto me, not necessarily trying to hurt me or give me suffering. All the incidents and conflicts with others happened so that I could understand my super defensive behaviour, and I attracted people like me. They were all strong and had exceptional survival skills.

Grief Is Relief: Returned Soldiers

Our ancestors – we, in past and present lives – have all been warriors, and we fulfil our role by fighting to survive throughout our lives. We do not bring back peace just because we win a battle. Our pain and anger remain, and we are exhausted for a long time.

'What were these battles all about?'

'What did we gain by sacrificing our lives, fellow warriors and families?'

'What did I do for the love of my family and country?'

'Was what I did for the love of my family and the country justifiable?'

'If I stop being a warrior, what am I?'

'How can I live without fighting?'

'What does it mean to create my life based on abundance, bliss and innocence? How? And is it possible?'

When we stopped fighting, the feeling of emptiness turned into pain. The pain turned into anger against the 'love' for the collectives. We may have been furious that our love for our family maintained the structure. We may have felt a sense of loss and exhaustion even though we were no longer fighting. All we knew was that we had to be strong to survive. That gave us a sense of living and purpose in life. 'Without fighting, how can we protect our loved ones?' 'Without fighting, how can we give meaning to our lives now?' We did not know how to live without being a warrior.

We have all been deeply disappointed in the illusion that winning a war will bring peace. Whether the battle was won or lost, everyone was in despair, having lost our loved ones, human connections, human dignity and self-trust. Even though we fought to protect our loved ones, the fear of being attacked and the guilt of attacking and hurting people haunted us. The internal war did not end even after the war.

Even if, for self-defence, we attacked our enemy and blamed them for their attack, we could not justify the fact that we hurt them. It may be justifiable in the belief of survival, but not in our hearts and our true essence. We could not forgive ourselves for what we had done to survive. However, holding onto the guilt and shame cost so much because it kept us stuck in darkness and did not allow us to live in this moment. Guilt and shame would not allow us to mourn the warrior within and understand those who have fought to survive throughout their lives. We have tried to make peace with ourselves by understanding what really happened to us, letting go of it, and returning to our true selves.

By understanding warrior energy, we can resonate with the challenging lives and experiences of warriors and ancestors. Eventually, we can let go of the energy and make peace within ourselves.

Without learning about our trauma, we would not have understood the cause of the emptiness, pain and anger from losing the connection to our true essence.

By understanding the warrior energy, we can soothe our souls and those of the deceased warriors (ancestors) who continued to carry the pain and isolation even after their death. We can mourn and grieve our loss through all the battles, and finally, we can free ourselves from the prison of pain. Ultimately, we can relieve ourselves from the belief of 'peace' we thought we would only obtain by fighting.

We are returned soldiers after a long period of fighting. We are learning to create and live in a new world where the struggle for survival no longer exists and allows us to emerge as our true selves.

Our Long Healing Journey

Throughout human history, we have thought that being strong is everything. We believe it is how we can change ourselves, others, and the world.

Because of our determined warrior energy, we can face and triumph over our life challenges. On the one hand, our determination contributes to persistently healing and learning from our traumas over all these years. On the other hand, because of our ability to achieve what our minds are set to do by suppressing our feelings and emotions, even though healing is a process/journey of reconnecting those vulnerable initial feelings, we focus on only completing the mission of 'healing'. We have the attitude of 'no matter what, we heal, and we will achieve the goal.' In other words, our focus is always on the future result rather than being in the moment and expressing how we feel.

We regard our vulnerability as troublesome for getting the job done. It is dangerous to our existence and the enemy's weakness. Since we automatically shut our hearts down, those warrior characteristics become the biggest obstacle to our healing journey.

We want to identify our feelings and emotions, which are the seeds of recreating the situations and circumstances we feel we must keep fighting. And yet, as soon as we sense those are about to appear, we consider them chaotic situations. Therefore, we attack or suppress those feelings and emotions as a reflex. It becomes a self-attacking program.

The warrior energy reminds us of gatekeepers who cannot leave their position: they are in a dilemma between watching the enemy and protecting their wife and child simultaneously. Moreover, their loved ones need their care and ask for their attention, but they must silence these loved ones so they are not attacked. They believe the voices of the vulnerable and innocent are too dangerous to all.

As a result, healing ourselves requires tremendous patience and determination due to the self-attacking program: our minds have their own interpretation of healing and habitual mechanisms, which differs from how actual healing unfolds. Hence, we often feel stuck in the journey.

After all, all we can do is heal what we can deal with at that moment when our trauma calls for our attention, even though we feel like nothing is moving forward or changing. In other words, we must learn to allow our hearts to take us to where we need our attention for healing: we need to stop letting our minds decide. We are required to surrender to them for our healing.

Problem, Reaction and Solution Program

Love empowers you to trust your power to create your life. You are the creator of your life and your world.

However, since we consider ourselves incomplete and not good enough, we regard ourselves as a problem to be solved. We project the self-perception onto others. We see everything and everyone as an issue to be solved. Focusing on solving problems means we constantly need problems. In other words, you need to be a problem in the first place. The perception that *I am the problem* is the seed of another illusion. It is just a belief, but we are busy solving problems that are often not problems in the first place. Eventually, solving problems becomes life itself.

We look for 'solutions' from outside ourselves. Solution providers are everywhere. Businesses, academia, spiritual gurus and all others attract us to 'solve' our problems. We even need inspiration from others to try to inspire our 'incomplete' and 'lacking' selves.

Because we see everything as a problem, even though the solutions already have potential 'issues', we believe solutions from outside ourselves would sort out everything. Thus, we perpetuate the search for solutions provided by others.

The authorities function and make a living by providing solutions to the 'problems' they create, where there are no problems to begin with. They need to show that they are a saviour for us, as if they represent our interests. Without problems, the importance of their existence would be questioned. Therefore, they have to keep creating problems to bring up our fear, primarily through the news and media. These are their self-performing skits.

This makes our minds focus on issues and fear what is happening. We believe we could feel 'safe' by hoping to get solutions from others.

But the sense of 'peace' is only for a moment. This is the pattern of the Problem-Reaction-Solution mind program, which is another illusion that we believe in.

This mind program does not allow us to choose how we want to see ourselves and live our lives. We are not free. If we do not set ourselves free from these limitations, we cannot create our lives as we wish.

On the contrary, we can receive and utilise resources others supply to create our vision. This creation is not based on a problem but on our freedom of choice. It embodies our essence of abundance, bliss and playfulness.

Projection of Abuser, Victim and Saviour Program

When we see people in pain and struggle, we empathise and automatically label them as a victim, someone who appears to hurt the person as an abuser and another who rescues the person as a saviour. We were in a structure and system based on an abuser, victim and saviour program for many years. It is a mind program that we believed in the old system. It was often used in religion, entertainment and our relationship with authority.

This belief separates us. Depending on the situation, we swap these roles among the people around us or with the mentioned entities.

We praise and idolise those who rescue the victims. The more we worship the saviour role, the more we emphasise the needs of victims and abusers. The saviour cannot fulfil their role without the other two roles.

Sometimes, you may consider someone as an 'abuser' in your life. Let's say, the one who triggers you. Often, those people give clues about your trauma and where to heal – every experience can be used to know yourself and to grow out of unpleasant situations and relationships. Furthermore, the abuser that you consider is the relationship you have with yourself. This means you are the one attacking yourself with the thought that the 'abuser' is attacking you if you consider yourself a victim.

In other words, because you become a victim by abusing yourself – for example, you keep saying, 'You are not good enough' – you attract an abusive person who materialises a situation that validates your self-abusive thought.

These abusers are hurting themselves. Self-abusive energy is projected onto others. Because they have been abused and traumatised, they attack themselves and others. They are disconnected from their true self.

What happens inside us manifests outside us and in all relationships with people. What seems to happen to you outside of yourself can often tell what is happening inside you. Relationships with the people around you are created based on self-perception and how we feel about ourselves.

When others' behaviours trigger you, you ask yourself,

'What belief do I have about myself?'

Because you attack yourself, you think you are a victim and ask for a saviour. This is how you create all relationships with anything and anybody based on your self-perception.

When you understand these dynamics and let go of those emotions and feelings that created this belief, you will not be affected by the 'abuser' anymore.

For example, someone abused you in your life, and you become a victim and seek a saviour who rescues you from the abuse. You see your world through the lens of you, a person who does not have the power to break this perception. You believe that you deserve to be abused, and you cannot help yourself out of the pattern, so you seek a saviour who always rescues you. This savour can be a person, drugs, medicine, 'God', and all other addictions. But by understanding this pattern, you will realise that you are the person who breaks this dynamic. Ask yourself, 'What happened to me to believe these dynamics and when?' Understand this initial incident and the dynamics of the people involved.

You do not have the self-abusive energy in you, so you no longer have the abuser's energy: something that does not exist in yourself will not exist in your outer world. Being truly you is coming out of the dynamics of the relationship and creating the world of abundance and bliss that you are. Then, you will experience others differently.

The Effect of Our Traumas

Releasing your hurtful emotions can only come from knowing that you are the powerful one who can heal yourself and change anything.

When you let go of a 'victim' energy, an 'abuser' and 'saviour' cannot exist.

When you let go of a 'saviour' energy, a 'victim' and 'abuser' cannot exist.

When you let go of an 'abuser' energy, a 'victim' and 'saviour' cannot exist.

The other roles cannot exist alone by letting go of one role.

No matter how painful your experience is, you can heal yourself with determination and self-love. The natural self is hidden under our trauma. However, it is too massive to be hidden by the trauma, and that is what we are made out of. Therefore, our essence can let go of the emotions and feelings that made us believe in this program to allow our true selves to emerge.

You are the creator of your world. We innately have all the knowledge and wisdom to change our lives. Everything you need is in you. No one outside of you has more power than you.

What you are currently experiencing can be extremely challenging, and you may feel like a victim of circumstance. However, please remember you wanted to know yourself by experiencing a transformation of the self-healing energy to your original state of abundance, bliss and innocence.

So do not wait for 'heroes' to come and save you because the belief itself is the program. After all, self-responsibility is self-possibility. We can take responsibility for our lives. Remember, you are the creator of your life and reality!

Why History Repeats Itself

Our history of fights and wars has repeated itself because the traumatised and programmed illusional self runs our world. Power and control are everything for our survival. The mind commanded the heart and inner child to stop expressing themselves and obey to maintain the power structure. When we create something, it is all for competitions and battles, meritocracy and survival of the fittest. It is purely for survival. Control and power maintain the hierarchical system and structure. The world co-created by us and the invader has been built by control and power, not from our natural self of abundance, bliss and innocence.

Therefore, changes, creations and rebirthing are problematic for those wanting to maintain the structure where we use a tiny percentage of our human abilities. The invaders and we all ensure we do not shift our self-perception from our ego to our natural state. Everyone becomes fearful of changes and chooses to stay in the survival world. Consequently, we have copied and repeated someone else's 'success' in the past to continue the system. We worship people with more knowledge, which sustains the system instead of valuing our experiences. We make our minds better than the heart and inner child, so the mind does not give importance to information from them, and it solely functions without communicating with them. When the programmed mind decides and runs everything by itself, it only does what it knows from the past and applies it to now and the future; it only functions as statistics. They function only on probability, not possibilities. Thus, there is no creativity.

History no longer repeats itself when our mind surrenders to our heart and inner child. We create our lives from abundance, bliss and innocence.

Is your mind listening to the heart and inner child? Or do you keep doing what you know already? Change can be possible when you discover what hinders change in your life. What incident caused you to think that change is problematic, even though change is absolute?

No One Can Stop the Life Force

Our primordial desire is to manifest our true selves through our bodies, minds, hearts and inner child. The life force flows and vibrates through our bodies and all that is. It manifests with constant changes, creation and rebirthing. This brings greater awareness of ourselves. This is the power to create our life and world. Manifestation of ourselves comes together with changes. No one can stop changes. They allow us to embody our natural selves rather than forcing them with great effort.

The invaders did not have a life force but desperately wanted to 'own' it. Even though they tried to capture it, they could only access a tiny part of a snapshot. Even if they accessed the small part, as soon as they wanted to own it, the aliveness of the small part disappeared. What they captured was already dead. They could never own a life force.

Because they could only capture the tiny dead part, the system and structure they built did not change, grow or learn; they just repeated the same survival game throughout history based on the snapshot of our creations. There was no change or creation in the world that they and we co-created.

'Owning' is TRYING to capture the life force and to stop our never-ending manifestation with changes and creation. However, it is impossible, and they knew this. They knew they could not stop the fact that we continue to change.

What they could only do was influence our minds to believe their created illusion, which is the concept of 'ownership'. They were powerful only in the realm of the illusion, and we believed in their illusion and volunteered to co-create the world with them.

We can also stop co-creating the world by letting go of the belief. It is our choice; we do not need to follow the belief.

Chapter 3

What We Believed To Be True

Illusion of Ownership

After the invasion, the concept of ownership was introduced. They treated us as slaves, as if they owned us. We also allowed ourselves to be treated as slaves. This experience throughout human history has haunted us. The fear controlled us in any decisions we made, and life became about avoiding the worst-case scenarios rather than thriving. We saved and secured anything for those potential bad days. We held onto everything for future crises or catastrophes, although we did not know if they would ever come.

Due to our unawareness of our natural state, we feel a lack of love. We think that we are not loved. We believe in 'the lack of' all the time; we are endlessly unable to feel *enough*, but we still keep trying to make sure we have *enough*. We have lost the sense of trust in ourselves, life, the collectives, and the power to change the dynamics of our relationships with everything around us. We suffer from a 'never enough' cycle. We continuously take as much as possible from ourselves, people and Gaia. We become slaves to the belief of 'the lack of'. This has resulted in consumerism.

The invaders introduced the illusion that everything was ownable, and we believed it. In fact, we can manifest abundance because it is our natural state. However, the invaders can only manifest a sense of lacking and incompleteness because they are parasites. This resulted in the invention of the idea of 'ownership'. The feeling of the lack was precisely what they were, and they projected this onto us.

We are here to experience, but we cannot own anything. Our bodies exist to experience ourselves, not to be owned for trade. We cannot take it with us after our death since our body goes back to the soil, nature and Gaia. Our human life unfolds on Gaia while we are here. You are welcome to use anything while you are here, but you will leave all physical things behind when you die. You can use all the resources on Gaia to experience your life, but we cannot own them.

You may think all living beings, like plants, fruits and animals, belong to you because you purchase and consume them. However, they all have a life force that is the same as ours. In other words, they are us; we are all made out of the same thing, so it can be said that we are them, and they are us. There is no separation among all. There is no hierarchy in the importance of all our existence. All living beings are vital to us and to one another.

Money was invented as a means to 'own' because ownership is an illusion; even if you save money for your whole life and purchase a piece of land, you still do not own it. Since the land is a living thing, you are paying your money to the middleman between nature and us, who could not even own the land in the first place for the right to use it. It all started with the invaders claiming they 'owned' the earth. It was just a claim, not real. You are also buying the illusion from them. For nature, money has no use. This transaction was made without all living beings who did not claim their ownership and, in fact, did not have a concept of ownership. They just existed on this earth. We cannot cut off and separate networks of microorganisms, trees and plants on the land into pieces by claiming 'ownership'.

Because ownership was an illusion, how much we 'own' was just for a show of power or where we were positioned in the hierarchy. The motivation for it was coming from 'not enough'. Therefore, the power from the ownership did not have substance, so it was also an illusion. Money was used as a means to support all the illusions and to maintain the hierarchy of power.

Money

Money is used to make us believe we are not creative and powerful without it. We think everything would be sorted out by obtaining and possessing more money. The feeling of lacking propels us to want more, as if we could gain love from its power. We trap ourselves and keep running on a money-making treadmill, not knowing that the actual cause is the lack of self-perception as abundance and completeness, not the lack of money.

In addition, the ego, an illusional identity, is based on feelings of lack and incompleteness. Furthermore, it misunderstands power and freedom. We interpret power as the ability to do anything we want with money, even though we may harm ourselves and others. We think that the more money we have, the more power we have. Even more, we believe this is freedom. Thus, we become obsessed with money because money is 'promised' to give us power and freedom.

Money works well in hierarchical relationships. The power hierarchy separates, conditions and controls us, and money is a means and measurement to support the system.

However, we still always feel insufficient in any situation, so we think we need more power to do anything all the time. Hence, we cannot fill in the emptiness of the lack and incompleteness.

We are taught we need money not only to survive but also to manifest our abundance. We even think we can only have our hearts' desires and freedom once we have enough money.

Many people sacrifice their desires and freedom to survive for money. We do not even allow ourselves to want what we desire. We believe we are not worth manifesting our desires or freedom if we do not have enough money. We think that only when we have more money can we have 'freedom'. However, even though you have more money, because it supports the illusion of 'ownership', it becomes only an accumulation of another illusion. True power and freedom – manifesting abundance, bliss and innocence of our natural state in this physical world – are not attainable, and we feel emptiness from the lack and incompleteness again.

Our true power is manifesting our true selves through our own creations. We manifest resources to realise this because we are abundant in the natural state. Our natural state is the source of our creations. Therefore, the mechanism of manifestation has nothing to do with having money first. The law of manifestation works the other way than what has been told.

Living our lives depends on our free expression. When we are not expressing it, our aliveness dies, and then we think we need money to regain our aliveness.

Then how about our death? Does it have anything to do with money? Our bodies die when we are ready to leave this world. Does money make you die peacefully? How you die depends on your beliefs and perspective of your death. Our life and death have nothing to do with money.

After all, money does not have a heart we can resonate with because it is not a living being. Money alone does not birth anything. Money comes between our relationships with everything, often to control us and make us slaves to it because we believe it to be the case. It has power only within the belief of 'ownership', which is an illusion.

Even if you could influence a situation or experience things you want by using money, your abundance manifests it. It is you who has power, not money.

We cannot measure and value our joy and abundance with numbers. Joy is just joy. It is your heart singing and your body dancing. It is what makes you giggle. There is no high-value joy or low-value joy.

Appreciating ourselves is self-love, which has uncountable value and power. Furthermore, our abundance is different from the amount of money that we have. Our abundance is the ability to manifest uncountable possibilities and experiences, not only in terms of money.

The power of joy is phenomenal. Your joy influences your family, friends and community, echoing your universe. Remember, because you are the creator of your world, when you create relationships with everything and everybody based on joy, whatever you create in your world is a manifestation of your joy.

For now, we are using money. However, money diminishes its power and importance because we start valuing and appreciating ourselves and realising our true power and value.

We lived when our self-value and self-power were inverted to the illusional value and power of money.

Hierarchy of Power to Communities Without Hierarchy

The hierarchy was used to separate and control people. It was twisted into the power structure by creating different socio-economic classes and adding money and knowledge as measurements of power.

They created the lowest class – poverty, which is unnatural to humans and Gaia – so that they could make the other classes feel superior.

Even though people in the class just above the poverty or even middle-income class are still financially struggling to fill their needs, they feel superior to or sympathise with those in poverty.

The hierarchy makes those in higher classes want to save those in poverty financially or academically by giving donations, knowledge or spirituality. These fundraising/donation programs and overseas aid are often used to create an image for those needing recognition or 'saviour fame'. Indeed, some people's untiring efforts and genuine intentions have changed the lives of low-income people.

However, it is still only a Band-Aid effect because the disparity is intentionally built into the inverted hierarchical system. Thus, the changes are small. After all, helping people in poverty is possible depending on the success of the pyramid system, which we praise for its competitiveness and meritocracy, solidifying economic and social disparities. Little has been done to change our system itself to eliminate poverty or extreme differences in accessing resources.

We all feel superiority from being in a higher class and inferiority from being in a lower one simultaneously. In other words, the co-dependency between superiority and inferiority has sustained the hierarchical structure.

Superiority: We do anything to avoid falling into the poorer class that we look down on, are ashamed of, and want nothing to do with by continuing to make more money or gain more knowledge. We also think we need to save those in poverty because we believe they are incompetent.

Inferiority: On the one hand, some of us have hatred and anger towards those in a higher class. On the other hand, others admire the higher class. Some climb towards the higher class and join in by working hard and making connections to gain a better status. Others become complete slaves to their ego. This makes us feel superior to or more 'fortunate' than the people in the class where we used to be. Some of us become 'heroes' who save the poorer where we once belonged by contributing to them or teaching them 'how to' move up towards the higher class in the pyramid, where we think we have more opportunities and a better life.

We feel inferior when we are in the lower class, but we feel superior when we join the higher class. Superiority cannot exist without inferiority, and the reverse is also true.

Ultimate poverty: This class was specifically made for those in all other classes to run the pyramid system efficiently and solidify it by making them always feel superior to the ones in ultimate poverty. In this class, we give in to the power structure or accept our situation, thinking, 'because it is the way it is', like Karma. Therefore, we accept where we are and submit to the situations of our lives.

How about the ones in the highest class in the pyramid? We can buy the illusional 'freedom' and 'power' as high-class members. It is a rather exclusive membership. We were high-paid slaves who ensured that the hierarchy system was working. Our lifestyle and status were 'guaranteed' because we were born into families meant to sustain the hierarchical system. Because their sense of superiority over the massive number of people in the lower classes feeds our egos, it is more difficult to get out of the belief. We were the royal and highest-paid slaves under the direct control of the invaders. Therefore, we were abused, controlled and manipulated so much because we believed that was the way to survive.

The higher we were in the hierarchy, the more we were away from our natural selves by keeping our superiority and ensuring the pyramid system worked. The emptiness from obtaining the illusional 'freedom' and 'power' propelled them to want more, believing that the emptiness can only be filled by doing what we are currently doing. Some may have considered that the more 'freedom' and 'power' they had, the more they thought they could get true freedom and power one day, or others believed that was the only way to survive in the environment, because that was all we knew. Eventually, we lost ourselves and thought that this illusional freedom and power were the ones we were striving for. All they were feeding was ego, the superiority to the masses and the inferiority of being a royal slave who did not have the slightest freedom and power in their individual lives compared to the masses who had more freedom and self-power. We were in despair and had hatred towards the masses. After all, the hatred was towards ourselves.

The invaders advertised the fraudulent success story of owning true freedom and power by obtaining more money. This was the biggest untruth and another empty promise. No matter our class, we all believed it and created our world based on that illusion.

Whatever you do in your life, you can be proud of it. There is no hierarchy in who we are, what we do, and what we desire to do.

There is no low class and high class. No one is more important than others.

We are creating a community without hierarchy and middlemen between our relationships. The pyramid system has been falling apart. We can recognise the co-dependency of superiority and inferiority, which supports the hierarchy within ourselves, and can heal our trauma that co-created the co-dependency together with the invaders. It is the process of knowing who we are as the creators of our own world.

There will not be people above us to run our lives and tell us how to live our unique lives, and we will not be telling anyone how to live their unique lives. We are the only ones who know how to live our lives well.

Indeed, people are interested in certain areas and are usually very good at them. We all have a unique gift! We always have someone who enjoys doing more in the areas you have less interest in. That is the uniqueness. We all have unique gifts that we can share with others. However, there will not be a power difference. We are just sharing our joy. This sharing of our joy is an abundance of life that we have come to experience.

The change towards the community without hierarchy requires much more open communication than the hierarchy system had because we no longer have this hierarchical framework.

The Limitation of Knowledge and Teaching

Power is often measured by how much knowledge you have. Those who provide knowledge have more influence and power in society. The more you know, the better your academic and financial opportunities will be. Knowledge is often expressed through words. In some cases, you may not have any experience with the knowledge you provide.

Hierarchies of knowledge and teaching exist everywhere. Knowledge operates in this realm of acceptability. It controls what and how you express yourself, and your expressions need to be accepted in a circle that you belong to.

To survive, we need to be accepted. Therefore, we go to an information provider, such as a teacher or an expert with whom we resonate, respect or admire. Those people teach or provide them with what they believe is right, and they have authority and power in their field.

As beginners, we think we need to learn more about a particular area that the specialist teaches or shares information about. However, as beginners grow, they expand their awareness and challenge the expert's knowledge. This meant you were an outcast and would sometimes be punished, especially in academia or even spiritual circles. We did not want to offend the expert with our free expression. The students or those with 'less knowledge' did not want to free themselves due to the risk of disrupting the community to which they belonged and being expelled.

Because vulnerability is outside the hierarchical relationship, teachers or experts would not show it. Vulnerability allows people to connect no matter what class they are in the hierarchy because it is beyond being right or wrong as the roles of a hierarchical class. In other words, without vulnerability, there is no real human connection and understanding of self and others.

Some teachers may say 'be your own person!' but because their livelihood and role depend on teaching their knowledge to their students, it is more challenging to be who we are and to have real connections in the hierarchy where co-dependency between superiority and inferiority is inherent. Without a student, a teacher cannot exist, and without a teacher, students cannot exist. Thus, to identify ourselves, we need the other in this structure.

Even between teachers and students, if we did not resonate with each other, we would not meet one another. There is common knowledge that we want to explore between both sides. Through this process, students learn about themselves, and teachers know about themselves through their interactions with the students. Therefore, information and knowledge come from both sides.

One person's perspective triggers others to explore more, and this happens continuously between one another. That is the exploration process. And after all, knowledge becomes the result of the co-exploration of all participants. We are all part of the knowledge-exploration process and can no longer identify whose idea is whose.

Do all phenomena around you, your experiences and the people you have met and interacted with throughout your life need to be mentioned to show where the knowledge comes from?

Just because someone can access more information does not mean they own the knowledge. Knowledge is there; no one can own it. Indeed, some information can be accessed after a long period of determined and dedicated experience. However, it does not belong to the person. This is because everyone can gain the information when they are ready to receive it. When you are not ready, you will not receive it. Even if you know with your head, if you do not have experience, it does not mean you genuinely received and understood it anyway. Only your own experience can allow you to have the key to open the door to access the knowledge.

Therefore, there is no property that we can own as intellectual property in the first place. Knowledge and teaching have a direct effect on financial gain and protection for survival. Knowledge and education were used to maintain one's position within the hierarchy for survival or for corporations to expand and protect their profit. The concept of intellectual property does not allow people to express themselves and share what they know freely.

When a certain number of people start to access and 'discover' a particular piece of information from our consciousness, it is often a sign that the information will flow out and be shared with more people, like an avalanche. It is like switching on a part of our consciousness. This is the hundredth monkey effect. And this avalanche of information/knowledge cannot be stopped. This is why we cannot own information for a new awareness of human evolution.

We do not need to feel inferior to those with more knowledge because we all have valuable and unique experiences. Your experience is a vessel for receiving knowledge.

Due to feelings of inadequacy, incompleteness and a lack of self-trust, we collectively became hermits and wanted to be part of a community. We became co-dependent in the relationship between those with more knowledge and those with less. On the other hand, the information provider also projects these beliefs onto those with less knowledge, thinking they need help from the provider.

Since there are unlimited possibilities for our experience at any given moment, no one can tell you which is the 'right' choice or the 'wrong' one. We can only provide 'right' and 'wrong' choices in the hierarchical system. There are no right or wrong choices; we are free to choose anything. We only have an option to experience more.

We learn from our experience. The more experience we have, the more we can learn from it. Thus, we are our own teachers. Trust ourselves, who can provide everything we need.

Our knowledge was used for survival in the competitive world.

Holding onto a certain knowledge and teaching is stagnation. They are still snapshots of that time and consciousness. Knowledge changes constantly. We are all creative beings; therefore, we do not need to be insecure about others taking away our knowledge. You are the creator of everything in your world. No one can take it away from you. You just create another, another and another. You are always one step ahead of even AI. Keep creating! That is our true power!

No Middle Man

Since the invaders could not create anything alone, they used middlemen among body, mind, heart and inner child energies, between you and others, and between you and Gaia, to control us. These middlemen are money, media, academia, laws, medicines, insurance, all the agents, big corporations, the government, spiritual gurus and God. These middlemen maintain the hierarchy system.

No one else can create your world. No one else knows about you more than you. We do not need spiritual gurus to connect to our natural state. We are much more than all the middlemen can offer. If we discover that our natural state is abundant, blissful and innocent, we realise that we do not need the middleman, the system. They tried hard to cover up this truth with all their 'power'.

Our lack of self-trust from being disconnected from our true selves prevented us from communicating directly with each other. The invaders were afraid that if we established direct relationships, we would know we could live happily without the middlemen and systems. They did not want us to manifest our natural state. We projected self-judgment onto one another instead.

At all costs, they ensured we kept believing we were powerless and disconnected and needed to rely on middlemen. The invaders made the system highly complex with layers of deception so we would not quickly uncover the truth. With our minds, it wasn't easy to understand how the whole system worked. And once we were down the rabbit hole, it was so difficult to get out. Eventually, we went around the circle endlessly, finding the 'truth' one after another, as if we created another 'truth', it only deepened the hole. After all, we lost a bigger picture of what we truly were. The more we found what was wrong with the system, the more we disconnected from our natural selves, the bigger picture. The deeper you dug, the deeper you got stuck in their energy mud.

They were desperate to survive. What we believed to be powerless was the invaders' projection. All they had was the power of influence, not actual power, and we woke up to it. This is because abundance, bliss and innocence are our true forms. We can discern if something that is not our nature is not the truth. We have a reference to the truth. Therefore, we can see through what the illusion is.

The invaders used middlemen desperately to disconnect us from being connected to our natural state.

Our Inner Intelligence vs Legal System in the Old World

The legal system in the old world did not have as much wisdom as we innately have. After all, it is about crimes. It has nothing to do with how inherently innocent, empathetic and wise we are. We can overcome everything we encounter without judging ourselves and others, and create everything for our evolution. The laws were designed for the sole purpose of maintaining a system where crimes are inherent. The system requires 'good' people and 'bad' people to sustain its existence.

We do not need judges to tell us we are right or wrong. Allowing someone else to decide if our action is right or wrong has diminished our ability to trust ourselves. As we are sacred beings, no one else has authority over our actions. Being right according to the legal system does not necessarily mean being conscientious, nor does it help us deepen our understanding of ourselves. Being wrong according to the law does not necessarily mean you are deficient. Focusing only on right and wrong stops us from knowing ourselves and growing.

You may fear that the law of the system does not respect your claim and your fundamental human rights. You may believe the principle of nature supports your claim against it; however, conflict is not its essence. The principle of nature cannot be brought against the existing law as a substitute.

You are the embodiment of destruction and rebirth. The cycle of nature and the evolutionary process. That is the never-ending principle. They have nothing to do with right and wrong, crime or punishment. Punishment does not change people; it does not allow us to forgive ourselves and realise our true selves.

Because we project self-perception onto others, taking care of ourselves means caring for our relationships with others. Hence, it is indispensable for us to take full responsibility for ourselves. We can only be responsible for ourselves.

Words and being from your natural self and essence always carry more power than referencing written laws. You have the ability to transform your situation. Our heart intelligence, which encompasses our vulnerabilities and the elements of our natural state, provides the wisdom needed to shift dynamics in situations and relationships with others. Everything that occurs in our lives and among people serves to help us know ourselves and re-discover that we hold the true power as the creators of our lives.

Yet, the ego does not easily listen to our inner wisdom. Healing our trauma will allow us to listen to our heart's intelligence and manifest our natural self, effectively diffusing conflicts and changing stuck or challenging situations among people. This begins with trusting ourselves as the embodiment of wisdom and intelligence.

Chapter 4

Beyond Illusional Collective Consciousness

Fear Attracts the Fearful: How to Deal With Your 'Enemy'

I constantly had issues with people due to my own fear. My fear attracted fearful people by its resonance, and we triggered each other. I was looking for blame for my trigger. If I could, I often wanted to avoid people. At the same time, I felt lonely without the connection to the collectives. However, because I have embodied my natural self more by self-healing and understanding myself, I see their trauma, reactions, potential for healing, and inner gifts. Now, I do not see their behaviour as a threat. If I had chosen to stay in fear and deeply connected to the illusional collective consciousness, I would not have been able to see those layers of each person as a unique experience, but only see their behaviour as an attack against me.

The invaders have held power for such a long time. Even though they know that they have lost their power, they will not admit to you that they did wrong or repay you for your pain and loss. They will not give up fighting for their survival. They are desperate for survival. After all, their surrender, which is most likely not, will not heal you.

You did not know about yourself as a free being. You may feel how much they have deceived you, even though, in fact, you were the one who deceived yourself. You may be learning your rights as a concept, but that does not mean you are free. Knowledge of our freedom does not make you a free person. When you stop fearing a possible attack in your mind and feel safe within, you embody freedom.

They have known us since we were born and even before. They know your family line, personal and ancestral traumas, everything you do, and your fears. You cannot hide anything from them. The knowledge you gain outside of yourself cannot protect you from potential attacks in your mind unless you stop the thought of the attack. Your fear is the magnet of fear. If you let go of your fear, there is nothing to magnetise.

The ego tells us illusions about ourselves and the power of our 'enemy'. For example, we keep telling ourselves, 'We are incomplete and inadequate, so we cannot run our lives by ourselves. We must depend on the economic, political and social systems and structures run by "superior" people with higher education or experts and intellectuals. We believe that without the authority and the structure, we cannot live.'

Attacking your ego, which believes that you are incomplete and not good enough, is another trap, a self-attacking program. Do not attack or disguise your ego. Embrace it. Be friends with your ego. Get as much information from it about your trauma as possible.

Do not overvalue winning in the legal arena by believing that your justice will be served. This does not guarantee your happiness or heal your trauma.

Minimise time and effort for that. Live well. Otherwise, you are re-creating another trauma through this process and passing it to the next generation: you are teaching our children life as pushing and pulling between attack and being attacked. If you want to be safe, then stop your self-attack.

They knew their defeat, so they needed an illusion we believed in. They wanted us to believe that the ego is us, the illusional self, so that they could manipulate us well. Knowing our illusion is knowing our 'enemy'.

Begin listening to the information and knowledge the ego holds regarding all the illusions created based on our trauma. Learn about the illusions and let go of them.

On the one hand, egos are created to 'try' to fulfil what we feel we lack about ourselves with co-dependency, and they fear freedom. On the other hand, the natural self is abundant, blissful, innocent, fearless, free and autonomous.

Beyond Illusional Collective Consciousness

The fear of those with power can turn against our people. Fear never unites people; it separates them.

If fear does not run your life, you would not have issues with anyone in the first place because you do not perceive anyone as 'the enemy'. Knowing your fear will help you understand 'the enemy's' fear.

We often try to understand them without looking at our own. Then, we misunderstand or make assumptions about them based on our fear. In this state of your mind, you are making yourself a victim and making them an abuser. For them, your strong self-protective behaviour is a form of attack.

Self-defence can turn into offence. When you position yourself as protecting yourself, you automatically make others 'the enemy', and you are inclined to act aggressively towards them. In the other person's eyes, you are an aggressor. They are also doing whatever they can to survive and are desperate for their survival.

When self-protection heightens, you could be the one who pulls the trigger first due to your increased fear. The one in fear is more likely to start a fight.

They want you to be as paranoid as they are. They want you, the one with paranoia, to pull the trigger faster than them, since it gives a legitimate reason for them to attack you. You become an 'aggressor' in the eyes of the public, and that is the convenient choice for them.

The lack of self-trust as a free being will make you feel unsafe.

Nobody can give you this assurance of being a free being. It is up to you to embody it.

Your words must come from the core of yourself as a free being – your authentic way. You cannot rely on knowledge of your right as a free person to compensate for a lack of self-trust as a free being. Remember, it is just knowledge. The words become alive when you embody them. This means you are not a victim; you are not making them an aggressor or wrong. You are just stating who you are. In other words, you are not functioning from the idea of win/lose or right/wrong.

Winning does not make you a free person. Walking away from the dynamics frees you.

Fear exists in our minds. Fear attracts fearful people and events. It stops our evolution and creativity. If you let fear make all your decisions, you cannot create a community because fear will always divide people and attract destructive elements into your life, family, community and your world.

When you stop fighting against them, they have no one to fight with. All you see is their self-attack and destruction. Focus on your creations and diminish their influence. The worst incidences can often be avoided by realising your blind spot, which results in your reacting to your 'enemy'. Thus, your relationship with your ego determines the relationship with your 'enemy'.

Beyond Illusional Collective Consciousness

In the old world, we were all connected through fear. We believe we are living in the same world. We assume we think and feel the same way, centred around fear.

When we are in fear, we see everything through our fear. Even though whatever we see and experience reflects our fear in a mirror, it seems like we are experiencing fear from the outer world. Our trauma, the self-attack program, and the projection of the invaders all contribute to the illusion that we all live in the same survival world. That is the mechanism of the world we live in.

They ensure that we are all traumatised and continue experiencing fear, which comes from within but appears to look like it is coming from the outside world. Nevertheless, if we keep attacking ourselves with our thoughts, we will manifest them in the outside world. We are the manifesters of ourselves.

Due to our connection through fear, we fear one another and cannot connect through vulnerability because we think vulnerability is a weakness that people can attack.

In reality, you all create your reality and world individually. That is why we have different experiences.

Why do we see the same visions and have similar understandings about our world then? We are in the vibration of fear. That is the common resonance of all of us. As we are the creators of our world, we create a world where it is fearful to live.

When fear no longer governs your life, you are not connected to each other through fear. This means you will begin to operate from the vibration of abundance, bliss and innocence. This journey is inherently individual. You have been and will always live in your own world. You can only change and create your own reality. You may collaborate with others who share a similar vision. Even then, you have unique expressions and craft your own world. You are co-creating your world with others who resonate at the same frequency for our common interests. The same applies to others.

Your world is a manifestation of yourself. The fear we had separated us but gave us false connections. The actual connection that we have been eager to have was with our natural state rather than that with others through fear. When you connect with yourself, you live beyond mirroring each other with people around you through fear and do not live in the illusional collective conscious world.

Shame and Guilt to the Illusional Collective Consciousness

Shame and guilt to the collective consciousness propel the ones with those emotions to be saviours: we sacrifice our lives to rescue those who appear to be victims, the collectives. We think that we are the ones to wake those up.

Especially for those who are highly sensitive or empathetic, it can be very challenging to disconnect from the collective consciousness. Some individuals had to work for the invaders due to their psychic abilities, for their own survival and that of their families.

It is crucial to remember that we are not bound by any obligation to the collective consciousness. Just as our ego is an illusion, so is the collective consciousness.

As you created the ego, you created the collective consciousness. It was made out of you. You may want to understand the relationship between you and the collective consciousness and explore why you feel shame and guilt toward it.

In fact, by trying to rescue others, you are prolonging the existence of the illusional collective consciousness. By helping them, we are contributing to its existence.

The illusion gives us a sense of connectedness. Co-dependency makes us feel we cannot live without one another. Furthermore, it makes you stuck in helping others who may not want to change their perceptions, even though there are always reasons for people to be where they are. The invaders manipulated and heavily influenced people's consciousness collectively so that we would be stuck in it. This is another trap that we experience.

The shame and guilt we feel toward the collective consciousness are a self-torture program. You do not owe anything to others, and no one owes anything to you. Everyone experiences what they choose. We were in this relationship with the collective consciousness to keep creating our lives based on shame and guilt.

Especially highly sensitive/empathetic people feel strongly about other people's feelings and emotions; we feel responsible for the collective emotions and feelings if we have not healed our trauma. We become a magnet for emotions and feelings, and overwhelm ourselves. Consequently, we are stuck in the loop of 'I feel shame and guilt, so I am responsible for others' feelings and emotions', even though letting go of shame and guilt and disconnecting from the illusional collective consciousness by self-healing is indispensable to our individual world.

So, what was the purpose of the accumulated fear in the collective consciousness of your world, and how would feelings of shame and guilt towards it influence your creation?

The existence of the illusional collective consciousness made us freeze and get stuck in serving it by continuously feeling shame and guilt, and living in the world based on those feelings: we did not evolve by our creation based on our essence.

Loyalty to the Illusional Collective Consciousness as Survival

The more we feel disconnected from the collectives, the stronger our loyalty to them becomes. But it takes immense courage for us to be aware and break away from the reaction. Being loyal to a dysfunctional family, community and society is not a manifestation of one's true, authentic self. We believe that we will be loved and accepted in the community by our loyalty. We don't want to be excluded.

Living in our unique world and not conforming to society was considered weird. Furthermore, not fighting with 'the enemy' was considered cowardly or an act of betrayal, and not sharing the fear of the illusional collectives was called naive, ignorant and escapism.

Being different from the others was unacceptable, and in the fearful world, those in fear had power over those who had less. The one with less fear was always excluded, not heard, not taken seriously and punished. For survival, we had to be loyal to the fearful collectives.

The bigger group with fear swallowed those trying to be independent. Individuality was not promoted but hindered so that not only could the invaders control us easily, but also those with fear could control their families, communities, the country and the world. The ones who promoted fear had power. The free ones were nuisances to the power, so they were suppressed and penalised because they made others feel unsafe.

The more loyal you are to the collectives, the more valuable you are to the public. However, the truth is that the more loyal you are to the masses, the less value you feel about your authentic self.

Seeking the Truth/Justice to Compensate Injustice

Are you seeking the truth, what you are and how your world/universe works? Or are you seeking justice to compensate for your injustice, but you call justice the truth? Will the injustice be repaid for by you being right? If others or 'enemies' totally submit to your justice, does it help remove or heal your pain?

What if you use any means necessary to seek justice? That is how all conflicts begin; sometimes, we fiercely attack one another in the name of justice. Seeking justice hurts and damages others and, after all, yourself. This is because the other may not necessarily admit that they caused injustice to you, or even if they did, they do not care. They may say, 'You have done what you did voluntarily.'

Seeking justice to compensate for your injustice can lead to never-ending blaming of someone else. It is the perspective of being a victim and seeking someone else to be responsible for your life. It's a path that can consume your entire life. This prevents you from perceiving yourself as the creator of your life and your world.

You chose to experience all the events you encountered to heal the wounds you had carried all your lifetimes. At the same time, you also have the power to change your self-perspective as a victim. Acknowledging your illusions, understanding how your trauma created those deceptions, and transforming your self-perception can break you free from this cycle.

Your experience might have been painful and unbearable. However, you designed your life the way you experienced it to recognise your trauma and heal, but not to keep torturing yourself. Embodying our true self is realised by stopping the self-torture. These all happened for you to heal yourself. Therefore, seeking justice is different from the healing process and self-empowerment.

No one can do anything about your trauma. If you seek support, it's there, but it is up to you to take action. Do not spend your life chasing justice; otherwise, you will always see yourself as a victim rather than the creator. Normalising your trauma leads to endless pain.

The truth is YOU, beyond being right or wrong. You may ask yourself what makes you want to know the truth, and then you will know what truth you are after.

'I Deserve Success!': Success Becomes Justice as Revenge

Justice is often misinterpreted as deserving success in wealth and fame through business, academics, sports, entertainment and other arenas. Some believe success is compensation for the injustice they have experienced, as if saying, 'I will show the world that I was right.' Success becomes revenge for the injustice that we experience to the collectives.

The injustice we have experienced turns into shaming the others who made us feel that way. It started from fear against the collectives, and the fear turned into anger. The anger becomes revenge toward the others who made us feel shame for being 'successful' in the eyes of the public. 'I will succeed in business/academia, become famous and show the world what I can do!'

Seeking justice turns into making others feel shame. However, there is no guarantee that they will feel shame or guilt by your success being shown off.

In the name of justice, we take revenge on others, but revenge itself is built on the injustice we feel. Therefore, even when we succeed, the wounds from the injustice persist. We constantly oscillate between injustice and justice, and become far from having liberation from these perpetual dynamics until we heal the pain.

Then, what is the truth? It is what you truly are and how your reality is shaped. We are out of the survival game if we seek the truth through self-healing. You do not need anyone else to heal your wounds. Justice by success is another illusion we seek, and we believe we will finally become free. But it will never heal you and free us.

You may want to ask yourself if your success is to prove you are right.

We do not need to prove anything to anybody. Instead, manifest yourself by self-healing. Do not normalise your trauma. Otherwise, you will never get out of this dynamic.

Chapter 5

Blindspot of Spiritualists –

The Wounded: Healers, Psychics, Shamans and Spiritual 'Leaders'

Bringing Your Power Back

I desperately wanted to be healed. I spent over a decade 'healing' with spiritualists' teachings and techniques, believing they could heal me. I admired and trusted those who 'heal' people with exceptional gifts more than myself. I even wanted to be like them, and I became a healer at times. I attracted various spiritualists into my life. I still could not fully trust self-healing, even though I felt the healing went round and round, seeking one spiritualist after another. I sometimes put them on a pedestal because I did not know self-power.

Due to the resonance of both our trauma and the lack of self-trust, we re-encountered one another again in this lifetime so that we had an opportunity to recognise our pain. It was not so much their teachings or psychic abilities but their trauma that unveiled my unconscious trauma. Sometimes, the energy of our trauma is expressed louder than what we say we are on the surface unconsciously. We cannot hide our wounds.

I realised I misbelieved that those people with the gifts know me better and can heal me. This discovery set me free from this co-dependency and hierarchy: I embodied more of the true self who trusts the self. My strong desire to know the truth about healing resulted in self-healing and accessing the information in this chapter.

The illusions between spiritualists and those seeking healing have profoundly and vastly undermined the spiritual community. In other words, our illusions have created and sustained the illusional spirituality. The unrealistic expectations that we created among ourselves caused not only stagnation in healing but also disempowerment. The purpose of this chapter is to possibly trigger something in you to set you free from this spiritual paradigm and bring back your power to all of you.

Trauma of Spiritualists – Healers, Shamans and Spiritual Leaders

The ones who embody the truth, whose being is the embodiment of the creators of their world, know they are not bound by anything or anybody; they are not co-dependent with anything or anybody. The creator would depend on nothing and nobody, wouldn't they? Because they have overcome trauma, they do not project their trauma onto others. Therefore, they do not have 'enemies'. They function from the inner child energy, the essence of the earth's and the universe's creation, constant destruction and rebirth. They are living detonators of change. They have memories of our new world: they know they are the blueprint and the embodiment of the new world. They know they are creating this new world by expressing their true self. They are here to express the truth of themselves, humanity, the earth and the universe through them.

They had the unique gift of tapping into and instantly decoding all consciousness because they knew and understood themselves as the creators of all existence.

In this series of sections, we focus on the blind spots of unhealed spiritualists with potentially exceptional gifts who believe they can 'heal' other people and teach/preach spirituality to others. We explore what caused their trauma. I genuinely hope these sections will activate especially deeply wounded healers, shamans and spiritual 'leaders' to ask themselves why they want to 'heal' others.

Self-Abandonment

As is commonly known, Indigenous people had strong connections with Gaia and everything in our world. We knew we were the creators of our world. However, we were removed from our families and adopted by families who were not our kind. Thus, we felt abandoned and disconnected from the community. Our sense of exclusion, loneliness and abandonment propelled us to be loyal to the adopted family and community to fit in.

We have not been able to use our gifts: our connection to all existence, our ability to feel everything and everybody, our intuitive ability to know the truth and the illusions, and our embodiment of constant change. Because we were beyond belief systems, our existence was destruction and birth itself. Therefore, we often encountered very 'disruptive' situations and circumstances because we were living detonators of change. Those situations were necessary to destroy stagnant situations and birth new ones.

However, people around us did not explore the truth. They wanted to avoid discovering who they truly were or how their world could be created. Searching for the truth was unnecessary, or they thought it could endanger them. Thus, being an authentic self was a burden of sin and shame. We felt like we were cursed and denied our very existence because of the gift.

In this environment, we had to suppress our authentic selves and be like others. Our natural abilities were turned into survival skills, such as reading other people's energies, changing our vibration according to the situation and the person we were dealing with and manipulating the vibrations of others. Being like a chameleon who could change colours to adapt to various demands and situations was required for survival. In other words, we became highly reactive to others' energies and environment and forgot who we were and what our gifts were for. Thus, those abilities became our survival skills.

Additionally, we were exceptionally susceptible, empathetic and psychic. Still, some were unaware of themselves and what was happening due to a lack of self-awareness of this reactive tendency from our unhealed wounds. Therefore, we often got overwhelmed by our surroundings, or even the 'skilled' ones struggled with using their gifts. Without self-healing, our gifts would not be used effectively or even discovered at all.

To fit into the community, we became utterly loyal to it. We needed to disconnect from all our creations and, after all, who we were as abundant, blissful and innocent creators. We suppressed who we were as the embodiment of change – freemen. We stagnated by being loyal to the community and for survival and became the most prominent supporters of maintaining this system, the illusional collective consciousness.

Extreme Loyalty to the Illusional Collective Consciousness

Due to our sense or memories of self-abandonment in a past lifetime(s), we repeat a similar experience even in this lifetime. We have felt excluded, isolated, lonely and abandoned. To feel connected and accepted, we believe we must show how valuable we are to the family and community.

Due to these emotional experiences, we want to make ourselves indispensable so that we will not be abandoned. We are willing to do anything not to feel the pain of abandonment again, even though we have already felt self-abandonment all this time.

Because of our gift of energy-reading and energy-altering abilities, we have trained to be exceptional psychic warriors, gurus in the spiritual worlds or skilful healers and shamans as protectors or saviours who enslaved ourselves for the community sometimes in the past and present lifetime. It is like, 'You see, I work brilliantly. You can't abandon me because I am important to you and this community!' We are trained to work for the power in the name of 'love' for the collectives. We need them to want us. That is the only way to feel the value of our existence and be 'loved'.

To keep us loyal to their power and hierarchical system, they abused and tortured us to submit to them. Because the exclusion felt from their self-abandonment, together with the abuse and torture, were different experiences from others, no one in the community could resonate with us. Therefore, we could not share our experiences with anyone, resulting in even more isolation.

The fact that our trauma was not understood and not being accepted for who we truly are brought about self-abandonment. We began to believe that we were what they told us we were. In other words, we became the projections of the others and the power.

To be a saviour and protector of the community, we fought, hurt and damaged the lives of others, which also resulted in shame and guilt. We faced battle after battle and were constantly in crisis and intense situations. Due to self-abandonment and disconnection from our light, our essence, we began to believe, 'I am the dark.'

Self-Belief: 'I am the Darkness'

We, those who function from the inner child energy, the essence of the earth and the universe, with constant destruction and rebirth, are manifesters and creators, so we are chaotic in a creative way. The invaders need those people with the power of creativity to be under their control. They need us, the hosts who constantly create for them to survive as parasites.

We have to serve the invaders by using our psychic abilities to survive. Working for the invaders secures our positions in the hierarchy. We are involved in unpleasant work. We are also abused and controlled by parents, family, other outside agents and the invaders themselves. To serve the invaders, we have a duty to maintain the tradition of the power hierarchy. Or we are usually born into a dysfunctional family where abuse and control were constantly happening in our past life or maybe still are in it now in this lifetime. Because of our substantial influence on the collective consciousness, our bloodline is chosen to be under the direct control of the invaders.

Our harsh environment and unceasing crisis in our lives were the result of our traumatised self-perspective. These constant challenges make us believe, 'I am the darkness. I am the source of all the issues!'

At the same time, we often encounter very 'disruptive' situations and circumstances because we are living detonators of change, destroying stagnations and birthing new ones. We are the living principle of the universe that cannot be stopped. Thus, our nature and the invaders' interference resulted in a constant 'crisis'. Not only could they not stop it, but we also could not stop this evolution process – continuous self-metamorphosis. Resistance to this nature of our truth also caused even more pain and self-destruction. Acceptance was all that was: we cannot deny our nature and power.

The invaders could only slow our evolution by feeding off our energy for a certain period. Our evolutional force was always the eternal truth and ultimate power.

We still felt the injustice of what happened to us, and we felt shame and guilt for causing pain to others because of our duty and survival despite feeling we were victims. Beyond everything, we felt shame and guilt for the inability to protect our loved ones and for betraying our true selves.

Simultaneously, the invaders undermined the shaman and healer family line that held the information on the earth before the invasion and put us under their control. We have a similar background of being adopted by families, not our kind, known as the lost generation of native people worldwide. We felt isolated and did not belong to the collectives. Wanting to belong to something and someone got so strong that it resulted in co-dependency: 'I don't feel I exist without them wanting us, and I made sure to make them need me by being magically super capable.' It developed into co-dependency between healers and those wanting to be healed, the saviour and those wishing to be saved. We took self-respect and self-trust away from others because we projected our lack of self-trust onto others.

We felt our darkness was too intense to face alone. Some have believed: 'Whatever I touch turns into a problem,' 'I don't feel safe about myself,' or 'No one can heal me.' This darkness has become a blind spot among healers and shamans throughout all lifetimes. It is excruciating to reconnect with 'the darkness' to heal ourselves. Therefore, we carry it with us and project it onto others through many lifetimes, not knowing we have the pain.

This blind spot itself often motivates us to become healers again in this lifetime. Because of our shame, guilt and loyalty towards the collectives, we want to repay what we did to them for our survival and be forgiven by healing the collective consciousness. Ultimately, we are the ones who desperately want to find our light by being healed. Still, we do not trust ourselves enough to heal by ourselves.

We unconsciously say, 'It is too intense to face it; I cannot do it alone, so someone, please heal me!!!'

Thus, people in spiritual circles have similar experiences and blind spots, which is why we resonate with, are attracted to, and meet again with one another. The blind spot becomes our projection, and we unconsciously see the world through it. Because of this, we tend to get stuck in the same perspective and cannot evolve beyond the co-dependency between healers and those who want to be healed. We stay the same without a deeper self-awareness coming from the courage to dive into the darkness.

In the worst case, we projected the deep darkness onto others in the spiritual community, even though we all met again to heal ourselves by prompting self-awareness with each other. Because we get caught up in being right or wrong, we become far from spirituality, which expresses our authenticity, where there is no right or wrong.

If we seek the truth – who we really are beyond being victims, saviours or abusers – and if we do not seek justice to compensate for the injustice we experienced, we can learn from our reaction in the relationships with those with the same blind spots. Your trigger may be pretty severe, but how we react to it shows us that we have a lot to discover about our blind spot, where our trauma resides. We initiate this process by diving into our darkness because, after all, no one but us can heal ourselves. 'Healers can heal others' was hope stemming from our lack of self-trust and self-abandonment.

Remember, we are living detonators of change, destroying stagnations and birthing new ones. We are the living principle of the universe that cannot be stopped. Healing would happen without being 'healed' by the healers. We heal ourselves according to this natural evolutionary process. We all need to trust ourselves, the living principle of the universe that cannot be stopped.

'Healing' Others by Shame and Guilt of Healers and Shamans

The one who has healed does not try to heal others because they know they cannot. They know they can only lead by example and share their actual healing experiences. They understand nature's way: we heal when ready and cannot control when and in which areas. In other words, we cannot plan our healing with our minds, either. We no longer wish to be stuck in the 'never-ending' healing loop. We want to create everything out of abundance, bliss, innocence and play.

Then why were we propelled to 'heal' others so much? What made us believe in the illusion of 'healing others'? Why did we want to save the world? Why did we feel indebted to the collectives?

We had traumatic experiences with the invaders. They used our gift of communicating with all that is and the ability to create anything from nothing for their power. Due to the gift, our feelings and emotions directly impacted the collectives. Our fear, and not only fear, but joy amplified the masses' one, and they fed on the energy we produced.

We felt guilty and ashamed because we could not save our loved ones and the community of our kind from the invaders; what we did to others, the 'enemy', for our survival, doing whatever the invaders ordered us to do or voluntarily thought we needed to do, and worst of all, self-abandonment.

We believed that healing others would forgive us and soothe our souls. Eventually, we hoped that these deeds would free us from shame and guilt. Therefore, we thought people 'needed' to be healed, and we believed they wanted to heal themselves. Our 'mission' was to heal them. However, we brought this belief from our past, not knowing that we projected our need for healing onto others. Our attachment to healing others often makes us blind to ourselves and avoid self-healing because our motivation comes from the unhealed self.

We meet other healers and shamans who have experienced similar trauma in their lives again because we have a particular connection with one another. However, we are often blind to our trauma, as they could be. Remember, our energetic resonance leads us to encounter one another.

Those who come to us may think our unique gifts can heal them due to their lack of self-trust, but we cannot. With our blind spots, we will not only be unable to help them but also undermine their healing, even if we come from 'good' intentions. Even if we understand our blind spots and let go of them, we still cannot heal them; we can only heal ourselves. Our self-healing would significantly influence everything and everybody around us due to our connection with all that is, after all.

Due to this blind spot, we think what we see is something other than ours: even though what we see is not their trauma but ours, we believe it is not ours. We cannot see other people's actual trauma.

Meeting with people who have experienced similar traumas can give us clues about our wounds, which is an opportunity for self-healing. Despite this, we may not notice that we have the same wounds and get triggered by the same things, and we cannot see the truth about ourselves. The ones who have not healed cannot know the truth about us because they have not seen the truth about themselves.

Therefore, this mirroring effect with people who share our energetic resonance needs to be broken down. Otherwise, we will stay in the world projected by our energetic resonance. We may keep one another in the never-ending loop of spiritual work.

If we fixate on our persona/self-perspective based on the role of 'healers' and treat those who want to be healed as clients who 'cannot heal themselves', the projection of self-disempowering creates a healing world. The disempowering belief is that 'I cannot heal myself; someone else who is better than me can heal me', and this is projected at others: 'They cannot heal themselves, so I heal them.'

If you recognise this never-ending healing pattern and challenge yourself to break out of the healing threshold, you may also trigger your 'healers'. However, this curiosity is not to be blamed because the trauma that caused the healer's trigger was already present before you both met one another. The fact that you triggered the healer is not your fault.

When you challenge your limitation, you may be confused about whether the wounds are the healers' or yours because you believe your healers have already healed. Most of all, you admire them for their healing ability and sublimity. You project saviours who exist within yourself onto the healers instead of looking at them as they are.

We become busy building our healing businesses based on our trauma-induced belief that 'we cannot heal ourselves; therefore, we NEED a saviour'. This comes from our lack of self-trust.

The loneliness and disconnection we experienced even propelled us to be saviours of the isolated and lonely people. This becomes the pitfall of healing services.

After all, the freedom we seek is to stop punishing ourselves by believing we must help others because of our shame and guilt about not fitting into the community and the profound isolation, disconnection, and self-adornment that caused us pain. In other words, 'wanting' to heal others is a SELF-torture program that keeps running the loop of the illusion of being able to heal others. Indeed, we are very empathetic, so making other people feel better makes us feel good. This can become addictive because it gives us self-value, and we cannot live without it, emotionally and financially. As a result, it becomes co-dependency between the healers and those who want to be healed.

Would you still want to stay in the healing arena once healed? We may ask ourselves: 'What is healing for in the first place?' It is for freedom! This also means you are free from healing and can create anything new out of abundance, bliss and innocence.

The healed embody healing by living our lives. We identify others' blind spots and encourage them to discover them, even if it takes longer to do so by themselves, only if they want to. We value our self-discovery. We will not tell those who may not even want to heal themselves to their face, 'This is your problem to solve.' We will not 'heal' them like 'magic'. We share our experiences with them so they can discover their blind spots and let go of them alone because we know that is all we can do. We know diving into our wounds and understanding ourselves when triggered is the only way to heal.

Wounded Inner Child of Spiritualists

The inner child has the power of abundance, bliss, innocence and curiosity. When the three parties – male energy, female energy and the inner child – are healed, dreams and desires can be manifested. The female energy decodes the inner child's desires and dreams, and the male energy helps the inner child's wishes and dreams manifest physically.

The inner child is driven by the principle of birth and destruction – a universal force. The invaders knew how important the well-being of our inner child was to our evolution and the reason for our existence. They wanted us to stop evolving by accessing universal wisdom. They wanted total control over us through abuse and manipulation so humans would not discover how brilliant we were. They hindered us from embodying its power by reconnecting with our inner child.

As a result, we began to believe that we were not good enough by depending on them. The inner child of healers and shamans throughout generations, who could potentially access that unlimited wisdom, needed to be traumatised and suppressed so that we did not activate human consciousness and all that is. They ensured that our inner child would be crushed to the extent that they could take advantage of our power. We also chose to suppress our inner child to protect our wisdom and power.

Due to our ability to directly influence the collectives, the greater our fear, the better for the invaders. Our fear travelled through the universe, making our world as dark as possible. As a result of their conflict and distrust, we experienced excruciating pain and loneliness when we lost the connection with our female energy, like a mother, and male energy, like a father.

In survival mode, the father and mother were disconnected from one another, and all three parties were separated. Consequently, the inner child fell into self-abandonment. Our self-trust in our dreams and desires coming true is diminished due to this wounded child who is desperate for connection with their true self, female energy and male energy.

Often, we do not know our state when observing anything or anybody around us. We do not know our wounded inner child filter. We can only observe the energy dynamics of the male and female energies from the inner child. Furthermore, our inner child blames itself for the conflicts and disconnection between mother and father and carries the energies of the two, forgetting who it is and what it wants.

The guilt and self-blame of our inner child regarding the disconnection, confrontation, polarisation and distrust between them, propelled us to feel responsible and make amends for this trauma. In addition, because of our connection with all that is, we even feel responsible for the disconnection between the male and female energies of the collective. This guilt also resulted in becoming a healer, a shaman or a spiritual leader who keeps doing what we do, hoping the two get along one day from our unhealed inner child's perspective. What our inner child initially wants to experience is creation. The wounded inner child who has given up on what they want becomes the blind spot in our lives, even though it is the key to our creation.

'Hope' and 'Faith' as Justification for Constant Sufferings

Our natural self is to be excited about this life on Earth – especially those who manifest everything from the inner child energy with powerful curiosity and a hunger for new experiences.

However, we have experienced pain and struggle instead. Because we did not want to disappoint ourselves anymore, we stopped trusting that we would manifest what we were initially here to do. We lost self-trust in our ability to create anything we wanted.

We focused on hope and faith to justify our current challenges. Believing in hope and faith drove us to keep doing what we did. It was too painful not to have meaning for what we are experiencing now, and we desperately needed meaning for it. Hope and faith were the inventions of humans from our trauma, and the invaders used them to keep us in the suffering loop.

We could not have what we wanted to manifest for a long period, even over many lifetimes. In other words, we hoped but did not live in joy. Joy was always over there but not here. Due to our long, challenging journey, we became comfortable with being in a state of 'hope' and 'faith'. The longer we struggled, the stronger our hope and faith became, even though hope and faith were, in fact, the symbols of 'giving up'.

This could lead to the fear that those who recite these words as their occupation would lose their jobs if people gave up on their suffering by self-trusting in their freedom. Furthermore, we did not believe we could give up suffering that easily. Even though we spent the whole of our lives trying to regain self-trust through healing, we could not heal ourselves or trust ourselves. Instead, we worshipped something outside ourselves, such as spiritual teachings and 'higher' beings.

Their job was to ensure people kept hoping rather than helping manifest what they hoped for. We did not want miracles to happen to everyone; we wanted them to happen just enough for people to believe in miracles and accept their current life struggles for hope and faith. We needed to show that only spiritual leaders like us could use this magic for miracles to happen so that our words have power over people. The invaders ensured that spiritual leaders would keep people stagnated and not evolve by co-dependency through spiritual communities for as long as possible.

Since we have been disconnected from freedom for a long time, if freedom manifests, we will not know what to do and what we indeed want. Without suffering, we would be lost. We could even lose our jobs. 'What do you want?' It would be the most confronting question for us. We fear our freedom because we are so used to the belief of accepting the challenges and suffering of life as the norm. Therefore, it is easier to keep doing what we do by believing in 'hope' and 'faith'.

We gave up being true to ourselves and living for ourselves, so we did not believe we could manifest what we hoped for. We would have to sacrifice so much to have it if we could. In other words, hope and faith killed living in a dream. They took away our ability to manifest what we desired at every moment. That was how much we were used to our darkness.

The ones who have healed would be living in a dream already, not hoping for the dream to come true. To heal ourselves, we had to break down the powerful illusions of 'hope' and 'faith'. That is how much our inner child, living in a dream, was undermined. We became slaves, masters of struggling and took the role of maintaining the system and structure based on fear. The value of our existence was to 'help' people, slaves to our roles in the system. Thus, living in our dreams was not the value of our existence.

We were in despair and sought salvation for ourselves – the truth. Therefore, it could be said that we need healing for ourselves the most instead of 'helping' others.

'Shaman': Elite Official Slaves Who Serve 'God'

Due to our connection with all that is as the creator, we feel everything about people and whole living things, so we feel responsible for others' pain, joy and emotional states. We tend to be a 'helper' rather than being who we truly are, a detonator for change. This becomes a never-ending helper who is the problem solver for people around us, instead of expanding awareness and bringing new energy to ourselves and others by being the change. We all forgot what it was like to be an unlimited creator. Since the invasion, we have chosen to be problem solvers, even though healing naturally happens when we are ready, by self-trust. We created jobs called 'healer' or 'shaman'. Consequently, we were stuck in the loop of healing.

'Shaman' is an official position. However, we are not necessarily fully aware of our connection to our true selves. We are very sensitive to energy. We read and manipulate energies for survival. We use the gifts in reactive ways. Our perceptions and decisions are reactions to what is happening around us.

We were no longer able to see the essence of everything clearly. This means that we could not distinguish between illusions and truth sharply. Despite this, we often became psychic warriors who protected those in the power structure and the system with these abilities for our and our loved ones' survival. Ensuring 'happiness' – fulfilling the expectations of others – gave us an illusional sense of security. The invaders used our reactive ability, fear for survival and love for our loved ones for their power and structure. We did not use our full potential to fulfil the joy of our existence.

Everyone can embody universal principles and manifest unlimited possibilities. At the same time, some people choose to be a more significant influence on the whole being in this universe, with the way of our being. They are a detonator of evolution by maintaining their connection with the inner child. Those people unconsciously and consciously activate and stir the collectives to reconnect with their authentic selves. No matter their life challenges, they do not entirely lose their connection with their inner child. They have the strength and wisdom to navigate their world: they function based on universal wisdom, not the knowledge of the mind.

We are driven by curiosity beyond the right and wrong coming from the belief system. We do not have judgment about darkness. Instead, we use our darkness as a tool or opportunity to experience and know who we are, because we even know we created it and co-created it with the invaders. We understand that we created this world to know who we are and experience ourselves, no matter how hard some experiences can get.

We can distinguish illusions from the truth because we embody the universal wisdom of creation. We can see the essence of everything because we are the ones who created it all. We are the catalysts of change, who always initiate the destruction of belief systems to birth something new when the old way does not serve us anymore.

Fear of Innocence; Fear of Freedom; Fear of Ourselves

Innocence takes it for granted that we can do and have whatever we want. There is no doubt about it. This energy is precisely freedom. Freedom is the unknown, and the inner child thrives in freedom like a fish in the water. However, the illusional self would not like the unknown, which is free. The illusional self likes things to happen as planned: they like routine and structure.

Before the invasion, we trusted ourselves, so we trusted others and the world. We were not on guard for anything or anybody. Our drive for all our experiences is curiosity. Because of our innocence and curiosity, we let the invader in and began to suffer a stagnant life due to our fear.

Change is absolute. Even if we had experienced the invaders' influence, we thought we could go on to other experiences whenever we chose to. We believed we would keep evolving. However, it did not happen… We did not know we would be stuck in the repetitive history for that long.

We felt and still continue to feel shameful and guilty because our innocence and curiosity caused us and humanity suffering. We began to consider innocence – which drives exploration, change and evolution – to be ignorance, naivety and even insignificance so that we would not wake it up to its power again. We kept blaming our inner child for the chaos, carrying the burden of what happened, and even thought we should be punished for what we did. We tried to be the solution to everything due to the combination of innocence and self-blame.

We believed, 'I don't deserve freedom,' 'I need to serve the collective or the power,' and 'I am responsible for the sufferings of others.' 'I prioritise others more than myself.' In addition, we were fearful of our innocence and our curiosity to explore. We feared our freedom and had given it up for a long time.

We no longer trusted our power to create our world. We became victims of circumstance, and we became problem solvers and preached to people to have 'hope' and 'faith'. We had nothing to do with freedom any more. We forgot what it was like to be free. We became experts in endurance in suffering with 'hope' and 'faith'. We contributed a lot to the stagnation of humanity.

We trusted things outside of ourselves rather than our actual selves. We can only rely on our mind's strength: we become spiritual only in our minds by learning from spiritual teachings. How spiritual we were was precisely how much we suppressed our authentic selves, especially how much our inner child has lost its essence and freedom by innocence. We lost ourselves. Not just lost… but we feared ourselves. It was a self-staged hindrance to freedom.

We hoped for freedom but did not trust in it. We manifested all blockages and struggles not to manifest freedom, so we constantly faced challenges. We projected it onto everything and everybody.

We were so used to being in the state of becoming 'free' in the future – stagnation. That is why we are good at being stuck in the struggles and preaching to ourselves and people about 'freedom', but we struggle with being free now. This means we have tremendous difficulties with being innocent – being our true selves.

Remember, we are connected with all that is, and we influence them.

For the collective and, in fact, for ourselves, what we can do best is not meant to preach to ourselves and others with our minds. Instead, we heal our inner child. This has a much greater effect on others and everything in our universe. We are the embodiment of freedom. That is the answer to our prayer.

The One Who Embodies the Truth

The seed of our existence always innately holds the potential for darkness. All humans in the past and present know we have that darkness and how to use it. Especially those who can potentially create their world with ease through the inner child's energy, and they know it even more strongly. Many of them are spiritualists. Darkness is not evil, sinister or associated with only suffering; it exists to help us understand ourselves. We have always been aware of this. However, the invaders latched on, fed off the darkness and kept us in a cycle of suffering and struggle. We forgot what darkness truly is and how to make it work for ourselves.

We often encounter very 'disruptive' situations and circumstances because we are the living detonators of change, breaking stagnation and birthing new beginnings. We embody the living principle of the universe that cannot be halted. Thus, our nature and the invaders' interference result in a constant 'crisis'. Not only could they not stop it, but we also could not halt this ever-evolving process of continuous self-metamorphosis. Resistance to the nature of our truth has caused even more pain and self-destruction. Self-acceptance is all that is required: we cannot deny our nature and power. The invaders could only slow our evolution by drawing energy from us for a limited time. Our evolutionary force has always represented eternal truth and ultimate power. What we lost was self-trust, but we are beginning to remember this clearly now.

Furthermore, our innocence, curiosity and self-trust allow us to explore and evolve regardless of our experiences. We do not fear at the core. We know we can change the situation or create something different because we want to experience something else.

Change is the norm. We are not obligated to maintain the status quo and do not need to ask anybody to change anything in our world. We know we are the creators of everything. We know everything we experience is our self-planned experience; at the same time, we know we have choices at every moment. We do not need to try to change because we are the change, and change is absolute.

We have self-accountability, are self-driven by our experiences and have trust that we would not have planned our life only as suffering and struggle. We consider any experience to be created to experience and learn about ourselves. We do not have 'good' or 'bad' experiences at the core level. Even the 'worst' experience, the core sees it as an opportunity to enable us to experience our authentic selves. We are grateful for the experience of self-existence, no matter if we like it.

We are aware of our inner child, who is behind the creation of our experiences. Therefore, even though we feel emotionally stuck and unbearable, we know we created the experience to discover its initial intention, the authentic self.

The inner child explores the unknown self and contributes new experiences to the mind and heart. The inner child does not like stagnation. When the inner child holds self-trust, we are unstoppable.

We fiercely protected our innocence as the most precious. It was sacred. Only innocence can tell what an illusion is and what is true: we can distinguish illusions from the truth. We experienced trauma, and there were times when we did not want to trust ourselves. However, because we knew that only the self-trust that innocence has can take us back home to our authentic selves, we trusted ourselves, people, life and our world. Hence, we could not fit into a fear-based society, the illusion. Without trust, we could not find the reason for our existence.

We felt so much bigger than our bodies. It was too big to feel like we did not even exist, as if we would dissipate ourselves in the vastness – that big! We knew the vastness of our freedom and the tightness of being in the body. The expansiveness was too big to accept as ours since we were used to the tightness of our bodies. The contrast was so great that sometimes, it was challenging to hold the space of the vastness of freedom while staying in the body that was supposedly meant to manifest abundance, bliss and innocence physically.

We felt we came from nothingness; simultaneously, we were everything – not only everything but infinite possibilities. Unlimited possibilities reflect our abundance – ourselves.

We knew we were bliss. It is the life force and joy of aliveness.

No matter how difficult life was, we did not give up on the joy of living because we knew it was our essence. Even though the world we experienced was sometimes unpleasant, we always wondered why we were experiencing the opposite of what we were. 'Although I am indeed free, why am I feeling stuck?'

When we are experiencing what we are not, we are experiencing illusions. Our connection to our essence made our life in the old world based on illusions – fear – challenging. We could not give up our true selves for the illusions and could not submit to them. No matter how long it took to heal our trauma, we continuously healed ourselves, and when we got triggered, we dedicated ourselves to understanding what was behind our triggers. We trusted we could heal ourselves. We kept walking through all the signal posts of triggering points as our creator self beckoned us to home – our authentic self.

At the same time, because of our curiosity, we wanted to know about illusions – what we are not and how they work – the mechanism of the co-creation of the invaders and us.

This awareness is the power behind all experiences, determination and perseverance in the old world. It is also the power that opens the door to the new world. We have finally arrived home. We are only responsible for ourselves. We cannot be responsible for anything or anyone. Thus, we do not need to feel responsible for the 'healing' of others.

Our being, just being existent, will change anything and anyone in our world because we are the creators of all those, and we always knew it! Now is the time to play like a child, as we always meant to be. Welcome back home!

Chapter 6

What Can We Do?

Self-Value and Self-Appreciation

We are learning to appreciate and value ourselves, no matter what we have gone through and how we are at the moment. We may not be able to do that due to unpleasant experiences at times, but these challenging experiences wake us up to our authentic selves.

We can never fail if we value ourselves, no matter how we are right now, and appreciate our dedication to discovering and reconnecting to our true selves. This is because the only success is knowing ourselves as the creator, and being the true self, is there. 'Success' and 'failure' that we believe to be true are the experiences of perception. In other words, they are not the experiences of our authentic selves. For our authentic selves, every experience results in the success of knowing ourselves. Therefore, even 'failures and mistakes' will reveal our true selves.

No one knows your journey well enough apart from you. Everyone has an unspoken story. Community, friends or family may not recognise your efforts and determination. Relying on others' appreciation, acknowledgement and value of your 'achievements' or efforts will put you in the never-ending cycle of wanting acknowledgement from outside of yourself and, after all, limit your potential.

We can value and appreciate ourselves now. You do not need to wait to 'achieve' something to appreciate and value yourself. If you believe that you will be content and feel peace once you reach a point of achievement, you often end up feeling lacking. Even if you achieve a goal you thought you would be satisfied with, the feeling of accomplishment passes quickly, and you end up wanting to be even more perfect because you already feel lacking. You always think you are incomplete, even though you are abundant, blissful and innocent to begin with. Perfectionism from feeling lacking results in our endless dissatisfaction. This belief is created from our trauma, and we are letting go of it.

We cannot remove the feeling of lack and incompleteness by filling in where we feel lacking and incomplete with more of them. What makes us think we are enough and complete is self-appreciation and self-value for us now, because you, at this present moment, are the only one and all you have. That is the only thing that exists and is absolutely real. Other than that, everything is an illusion.

You have been dedicated to knowing yourself along the way. Everyone is at a different point in the same explorational journey toward our natural self. Self-appreciation and self-value make the journey abundant and blissful in gaining self-insight.

Peace and Balance

Peace is trusting ourselves even in the unknown, even though we do not know why it is happening to us. No matter our experience, we love ourselves: 'I got my back even in the dark.' Self-trust is like carrying a torch because there is light as long as you have the torch/self-trust, and that will bring you peace on your unknown path.

Balance is the mind surrendering to the heart and inner child, not suppressing and shutting them up.

Peace is not about keeping a low profile or saying, 'Let's not rock the boat by expressing how we feel because we cannot change anything.' It is not helplessly following those in power. Nor is it the despair that leaves us frozen in fear, afraid to offend or be hurt.

This is rooted in our family dynamics, like 'don't make our dad or mum angry... let's keep the "peace" and "balance" of the family.' We continued to maintain the stability of our family power structure.

The invaders and those at the top of the hierarchy made themselves look like they represented the interests of the people and even the earth. Anyone who challenged the 'peace' and 'balance' of the power structure was called a traitor to the country and the community.

Despite our unfair conditions, we dared not challenge the established structure and the power to survive. The invaders used our powerlessness against challenging situations and hardships to keep the 'stability' of their power by punishing our freedom of expression as undermining the 'peace' and 'balance'.

Peace and balance originally meant surrendering to our heart and natural state. However, the invaders twisted these ideals to maintain their power, exploiting our despair and helplessness in the struggle for survival. The 'peace' and 'balance' that we kept served only to stabilise their power, ensuring our compliance rather than our well-being. They were promoted or praised as noble, sublime or spiritual, but in reality, they represented the total defeat of our own power.

Abundance At All Times: Infinite Possibility

Plants have the ability to grow, mature, flower and bear fruit, potentially producing many more seeds than the original. The journey of being an embryo, baby, child, adolescent, adult, and experiencing old age and death continues in human form. If the environment is conducive to growth, the number of seeds can increase by ten, thirty, fifty times or more, allowing each seed to undergo all the stages of life.

Plant consciousness explores itself through the experiences of each root, branch, flower, fruit and seed in this life cycle process. A seed desires to experience and learn itself through the changes. It has a blueprint for its experience and has a choice at every moment at the same time.

The eternity of the life cycle, the multiplying effects of seed reproduction, the evolution process, the simultaneity of the experience of plant consciousness through every part of the plant itself and the experience of interacting with other plants, microorganisms, insects and Gaia – there is the unlimited experience of the plant itself. Abundance is about the limitless experience of itself and is inherent in nature. Abundance is the truth about us. Our natural state is abundant.

Humans are made of the same life force as those plants and Gaia. The life force is to manifest and experience infinite selves.

The change includes the life cycle, the increased number of people in our family through reproduction, and the evolution of ourselves with all living beings. In addition to the change, we experience simultaneously relationships with all consciousness.

Since we want to experience the abundance that we are, we simultaneously manifest all our experiences of change and relationships with any consciousness. Therefore, in every moment, we have infinite possibilities for our experiences. This is abundance.

Our greatest suffering was that we always knew we were abundant and incredible beings at our core, but we experienced the exact opposite due to our egos running our lives. Yet, it was all for knowing that we are abundant. We all began with abundance, not a lack of.

Creating Your World, Not Changing the World

We all have trauma, so we have egos. We were all taught to judge ourselves. The mind program solidified our self-judgment into attacking ourselves. We mastered it so well to survive in the old world. We even did it unconsciously, 24/7.

We wish no one judged one another. We hope that we can live in a nonjudgmental world. We will eventually create it since we have been breaking the self-attacking program, the spell.

We always thought that others had attacked us. We all want to stop judgment, seemingly coming from outside. You may say, 'Please don't judge me or others.' However, they all judge, attack themselves and project it onto you and others. It is not yours in the first place. The same goes with us: our self-judgment projects it onto others.

A non-judgmental world cannot be created by hoping others will stop judging or by trying to change the external world. It is not about others' actions but about your own perception. When you feel triggered by someone's self-judgment, it is because you judge yourself in the same way. In reality, you are not being hurt by them – you are hurting yourself through your self-judgment. Your perception shapes your world, and only you can change it. When you break free from this mental pattern, you will experience a world without judgment, no matter how others behave. That is what makes your world liveable.

We get triggered by the word 'ego'. Judging the energy of the blockages that hinder you from connecting with your natural state would keep you in the program. Instead, the fact that you are getting triggered by the word itself is telling you that you may want to ask a question:

'Why am I triggered?'

After all, when your self-perception changes, your world changes. Then, all you see is egos as expressions of trauma and no threat to you.

By saying 'don't judge' to others because we do not want to get triggered, we are normalising our trauma. People judge themselves, no matter what you ask them, unless they want to stop attacking themselves by healing.

Your world does not depend on others. Your world is your world. Other people's self-judgment is theirs. It has nothing to do with you. Focus on creating your world, not trying to change the world that we thought existed.

When you are non-judgmental about yourself, people around you feel free to express who they are. By saying 'don't judge' to others, you are judging them by projecting your self-judgment onto them. Being free from judgment influences others to be free.

Manifesting Yourself

Manifesting ourselves is the only way to know ourselves.

Let's say we paint a picture… The beautiful harmony in colours in the entire painting is created by choosing a colour that expresses your heart and natural state at each moment. We may not know precisely what the result will look like, but we want to paint a particular theme. To do this, we experience various expressions of ourselves throughout the painting journey. Sometimes, our expressions surprise us. The surprises allow us to know ourselves even more. We can only know ourselves by expressing ourselves.

Our minds are programmed to have balance. We analyse and estimate where the balance is. The mind has its logical interpretation of 'balanced beauty'. When we are obsessed with the perfect 'balance' of colours in the entire picture, we become indecisive about what colour to paint every moment because the mind is not allowing our free expression. Then, this obsession with the 'balance' stops the creation of the picture. Painting itself ends up ceasing. In other words, we are hindering the process of knowing about ourselves.

But if you use a colour following expressions of your heart and curiosity of your inner child, every moment without obsessive thoughts of 'should be this, should be that' and without thinking of the 'balance' of the entire painting through your mind, there will be harmony between the colour you paint at this moment and the colours in the whole painting: the small parts are microcosms of the whole painting that is the entire universe.

Harmony is the mind surrendering to the heart and inner child, and manifesting our authenticity in this physical world. That is beauty. Harmony is the way to create a new world for ourselves. Our future is unknown, but we create it from our essence with self-trust. The manifestation of our authenticity creates the world we live in.

Everything and Everybody Are You in Your World

In the old world, we did not trust each other because we all mirrored our fear of one another. We felt connected among ourselves in the illusion of collective consciousness. However, the sense of belonging through fear resulted in co-dependency.

What others say and do has nothing to do with you. What they feel and do stems from their self-perception, which they project onto us. However, we thought they were attacking us. Due to our unhealed trauma, we recognise others' expressions as attacks. After all, it is our self-attack. This is how triggering happens.

At the same time, everything and everybody in your world is made from the same thing: you. Nothing that is not you can be created in your world because you are the centre and source of everything in your world. You are the creator of your world.

Your father, mother, friend, children, plants and the earth are all you. We choose our family, who show us our blind spots. The challenge is whether we use the experience with them to discover who we are. It is your choice if you want to do it.

Our closest people, like family, remind us of what we are lacking and our incompleteness every day, even though what they say or do to us is their perception. We believe what they tell us is who we are, and we get triggered by them. Our relationships with those people can be very challenging. Conflict with someone else is a fight within you. You are hurting yourself.

However, by interacting with them, you learn your blind spots and understand your trauma.

Furthermore, we can truly comprehend that you created everything and everybody around you to remember that you are the creator of your world. Then, those experiences become a gift.

To know yourself, you have created signposts in the form of events and relationships that reveal your trauma. These signs guide you along the pathways to your whole self, your natural state as the creator. The challenge is that the signposts often appear as obstacles or blockages. Whether you perceive them as signs or hurdles depends on how well you remember your initial motivation for your creation and your love for all of you. Can you love yourself as the creator who brought forth suffering and joy to you? Will you love yourself as the creator who designed all of this, so you can discover this truth? Only the creator's love for you and your connection with it is the truth, not the illusion.

Heaven is Here

Life and death are equally beautiful. Death is a part of nature's cycle as much as birth. However, we believed that the world was a dangerous place and death was defiled: we lived our lives concerned about possible death 24/7 and died with fear. Throughout life, from birth to death, we have a fear of death even when we are alive. You are the creator of your life. You are free to create your life. Despite this, would you still think that you created a life that makes you fear death for a whole life to begin with?

Our life is to manifest you as abundance, bliss and innocence. Death is to thank ourselves and our loved ones for the life we experienced together and bless our departure into another world.

Let's say no one knows what will happen after death. People who have died can only tell us what the world after death is like. However, if those people have died, how can they tell you about their experience after death? Indeed, some people would communicate directly with the deceased, or they experienced death and came back to life. Others learned that from those who have experienced death and come back to life. However, we are mostly told about the realm as a story by the still-alive people who have not experienced it. Therefore, it is always someone else's story, not your experience. Thus, they do not know, and you do not know! Then why do you believe in it?

The invaders made us believe that this world and the other world were fearful. Unfortunately, we created ego to survive on this earth, and our ego made our experience here like a 'hell' because of our trauma: we were alive, fearing death all the time. We put ourselves in prison for our beliefs. The invaders' promise for us to go to heaven after death through our good deeds was the way for them to make us listen to and follow them. After all, we made ourselves believe the illusion.

However, the most apparent thing we know of is that we exist here on this earth. How we want to experience life on Earth depends on our choices. We are free to make this place however we want.

Manifesting your natural self of abundance, bliss and innocence in any relationship – if it is possible here on Earth – sounds like heaven, doesn't it? You are creating a heaven in your world. Our child-like self is curious and loves experiencing unlimited possibilities. It is precisely the life force that we all are. The creation of Earth for this foundation was already completed a long, long time ago. Now, we are finally bringing back the foundation. We have been waiting for this moment since the beginning of our humanity. Come out from the cave in 'hell' if you are hiding. All we do here now is manifest our original self of abundance, bliss and innocence here on Earth individually, in heaven! It is time to play!

In Summary

We are much more than the ego, the illusion. Our journey was always about bringing back awareness of our natural state and manifesting our authentic selves. Nevertheless, we fell into a swamp of survival life on the path to home. If we say life is survival, we are admitting that it is ok to normalise our trauma and that life is suffering. If we normalise our trauma, we are claiming that we are nothing but the ego, our illusional identity. Moreover, when we criticise our ego, we criticise our traumatised selves: you are already hurt, and your self-criticism hurts even more.

We do not know what created egos and what they hold. Our ego is there to be understood. The story of the ego needs to be listened to because it speaks on behalf of our trauma, which overlays our true selves. Facing our trauma is the call from our authentic selves who want to be found. Embracing our ego and trauma will clarify the filter through which we have seen our world. Knowing the filter of the ego and how it was created brings peace within. Knowing that what we believed to be true was not true is liberating.

When you get triggered, follow whatever feelings and emotions arise because they hold all the clues to comprehend your trauma. Follow your heart and allow it to speak up to discover the time and event you began to perceive yourself as incomplete and inadequate. This is the journey to embody your true self hidden behind your trauma. This is healing.

Furthermore, it means that, as a by-product, this removes the influence of the invaders' projections, and you also learn about them and how they function. The invaders wanted us to keep believing that ego was our identity. They made sure that we continued to believe in our illusional identity, which was precisely the invaders' projection onto us as well.

Hence, our old world was built on our traumatised self and the invaders' projections. We individually heal our wounds, the seeds that created the self-attacking world.

In the old world, we did not trust each other because we all mirrored our fear of one another. We felt connected among ourselves in the illusion of collective consciousness through fear. However, the sense of belonging resulted in co-dependency.

Even though what others say and do has nothing to do with us, and they only project their self-perception onto us, we thought they were attacking us. Due to our unhealed trauma, we recognise others' expressions as attacks. After all, it is self-attack.

At the same time, everything and everybody in your world is made from the same thing: you. Nothing that is not you can be created in your world because you are the source of everything in your world. You are the creator of your world. Thus, when you learn about yourself by interacting with people with whom you have issues, you will no longer get triggered by their expressions. This will help you to realise that those around you are you in the first place.

Healing your wounds allows your natural state to emerge, and your authentic self begins to create your new world. The seed of the world is our natural selves, not trauma any more. You are free to make your world. This means we are creating everything from abundance, bliss and innocence that you are.

We are not used to freedom; therefore, we may fear freeing ourselves, and people around us may fear us doing it. This is an essential part of the healing journey. Why do we have a fear of freedom? It is because freedom can destroy our ego and the illusional security built by it.

Our life force is to manifest ourselves by experiencing infinite possibilities of ourselves. This is precisely the driving force behind creating your new reality. Your experiences come from your life force, which is your birthing power. In other words, you can birth various experiences of yourself in all relationships with everything.

It depends on you!

When we feel stuck in the same unpleasant situation, we may seek help from 'healers' or 'shamans', or they might wish to assist us. However, it's important to remember that we can all heal ourselves, and those 'spiritualists' are also dealing with their traumas if they feel the need to 'heal' others. We do not want to get caught in a co-dependent relationship between the 'healer' and the one who seeks healing. The healed only share their experiences but do not 'heal' others. They will not remove your essential journey of experiencing every layer of yourself by 'healing' you. They will trust in your self-healing power and watch over you.

You do not need to look for where to heal. The question, 'What else do I need to heal?' is unnecessary. When we get triggered, it is the best time for healing. Wherever we need to heal will appear when it requires our attention. So live your life and enjoy!

Finally, no matter your experiences, even if some were unbearable, you did not give up your power to heal yourself. So please appreciate how far you have come and value yourself no matter how you are now. Love yourself.

Understanding how our trauma formed can help us dismantle our illusory selves, which fabricated our old system. Embodying one's true self with this self-healing creates one's new world; at last, after a long period, we leave the old world behind. This becomes a pathway to Gaia Village, a new community.

Bio
Saeko Angwin

Saeko Angwin is an explorer of consciousness. She goes wherever her curiosity takes her by asking questions.

After over a decade of healing, she began receiving answers to her queries from her creator. Her interest in making a new community without survival, hierarchy and co-dependency keeps opening channels to wisdom. With these messages she wrote her debut book, *Gaia Village: Creating a Community by Embodying One's True Self.*

She was born and raised in Japan and has lived in Australia, China, the USA and Hong Kong. She currently lives in Sydney with her husband and children.

www.beyourtruecolours.com

www.ingramcontent.com/pod-product-compliance
Lightning Source LLC
Chambersburg PA
CBHW060457080526
44584CB00015B/1462